ADAM
COPELAND
ON EDGE

EDGE

ADAM "EDGE" COPELAND

ADAM
COPELAND
ON EDGE

ADAM "EDGE" COPELAND

POCKET BOOKS

New York   London   Toronto   Sydney

This book, one of my dreams, is dedicated to my Ma.

Words cannot express or truly convey what you mean to me,
but I'll give it a shot. Without you and your support,
my dream would not have been possible. With you and your strength,
you helped me believe that any dream can come true.
You are my true hero. I love you.

My fellow author, Mick Foley.

INTRODUCTION

A few years ago, I was asked to comment on my legacy in the wrestling business. As I thought about it, I realized that my peers opinions of my in-ring skills have relatively little to do with how I want to be remembered. Finally, I said I wanted to be remembered as a guy who made fans smile, and who was always good to the younger guys in the business. With that in mind, I believe that Adam Copeland, "Edge," is a major part of that legacy.

By the summer of 2000, WWE had been under attack for some time from critics who felt the show was too risqué and was inappropriate for children. I largely disagreed, and made it my mission to put a happy, goofy, innocent face on professional wrestling. Adam and Jay Reso (better known as his tag team partner, Christian) were my partners in this ridiculous endeavor. Together, our skits came to be known as Credgeley (for Christian, Edge, and Foley) and set the standard for hokey comedy and downright nincompoopery that should endure for ages.

Interestingly, in the midst of all the fun, E&C found time to tear the house down on many a WWE show, including that year's *SummerSlam* match, a downright brilliant contest that should endure for ages as well.

Alas, the good times had to end, as I departed the wrestling scene for a more hands-on role in fatherhood, and Adam and Jay received the crushing news (crushing for me, at least) that they needed to act more like real people. Real people, they were told, don't play kazoos.

Ironically, as far as people go, they don't get much more real than Adam Copeland. He is an intelligent, thoughtful young man, and an athletic, charismatic performer. He has sacrificed his body for the entertainment of WWE fans, and while paying for those sacrifices, found the time to share his story with us. The fact that he wrote it himself didn't surprise me—I always assumed he would.

His is not the story of an aged wrestler looking back on his long years. Not that there's anything wrong with that. I wrote one myself. Neither is it a story of a young Superstar reflecting on his rapid climb up wrestling's ladder.

Rather it is the story of a young man at our industry's crossroads. A story of an athlete poised at the threshold of greatness, who is counting down the seconds until a career-threatening injury is finally overcome by the formidable tag team of Mother Nature and Father Time, and then can team with a mystery partner known as Potential Not Yet Fulfilled.

As a wrestling fan, I can't wait to watch. As a friend, I will be nervous, but confident. As a mentor of sorts, I will be a proud couch potato and will always consider being asked to write the foreword to Adam's unique story as a major part of my own legacy.

—MICK FOLEY

ADAM COPELAND ON EDGE

by ADAM "EDGE" COPELAND

So here it is, my book. The life and ramblings of Adam Copeland. Now, if you have picked up this handsome little number, then you probably also know me as Edge. If you don't know either name, read on. Hopefully, wrestling and nonwrestling fans alike will be fascinated.

What you are holding in your hands has been a dream of mine. I've had many dreams come true, and I still have many more to fulfill. That's what this book is about: my life and working toward fulfilling those dreams.

You may be asking yourself, Why do I want to read about this? The guy is only thirty years old, how much of a story can he possibly have? Oh ye of little faith. These eyes have seen many things. This body has experienced things a body should not endure.

So now it's time to step through the looking glass and . . . come out on the other side. Okay, so now you are standing beside me. Not good enough. This is a story. It's supposed to take you, the reader, on a journey. My journey. It's my job to paint a mental picture for you. Theater of the mind. So here it goes, and bear with me.

Right now, faithful Edgehead, you are . . . a worm. Don't worry, this is the first, and last, time you will pretend to be a worm while reading this book (unless your name is Scotty 2 Hotty). You are now sliding your way into my ear (don't get stuck in the wax). Pop! You are in. Lot a room in there, huh?

Now it is time to truly see my life, through my eyes. The eyes deeply set under my Cro-Magnon-like forehead. Comfy? Here we go!

—ADAM COPELAND
Sitting on his couch in Tampa, Florida
(which has his ass crack permanently imbedded into it).

Are you okay, Edge?" That was the question WWE referee Brian Hebner asked me as I lay in a fetal position, pain screaming through my neck, the recipient of a Kurt Angle German suplex. I wish I could have answered yes; instead I spit out, "Give me a minute." The words I utter anytime something feels wrong. Really wrong.

Leading up to my match that night at the Bradley Center in Milwaukee, Wisconsin, I'd been saying those words far too much. You see, playing through pain is ingrained in a wrestler's DNA. This pain, however, was different and it was not going away. In fact, it was getting worse. One thing we don't have in sports entertainment is the luxury of calling a time out. The show must go on, and besides, I was wrestling Kurt Angle for the WWE Championship. I had been experiencing the pain for about a month. I continued to feel it for another month. Finally, I gave in, got an MRI, and discovered I had been doing all of this with two ruptured discs. In laymen's terms, a broken neck. I rested, I flew to South Africa, for a WWE tour, and back. I continued wrestling until I lost all the strength in my left arm and it quickly shrunk to the size of a noodle. It eerily reminded me of Mr. Burns (of *Simpson* fame) in a tank top.

Don't get me wrong; this is not a sob story. Barring the broken neck, I would not change a thing. It's just a look into the wacky world in which I make my living. It also helps explain why I had the time to write this book (in between episodes of *That 70's Show*).

My couch has a very Homer Simpson–like indentation where I was forced to sleep, sitting up, for seven weeks. It's also where I crafted this literary masterpiece (okay, maybe masterpiece is reaching, but you get the idea). So, while repairing my weary old bones at the ripe old age of thirty, I had time to reflect. This brought on my epiphany (actually it was my ex-wife's epiphany, but who's counting); I would write out my life story, in long hand à la the hard-core author Mick Foley, because, like Mick, I, too, am computer illiterate. I was undaunted though, because I was about to write my very own book, my life story.

This is when my first dilemma hit me harder than an Undertaker chair shot. How do I do this? Better yet, where do I start? Well, folks, I am still not sure if I know, but as I sit here at 2:30 A.M. in my underwear (not a pretty thought, I know), the very beginning seems like a good idea.

Yeah, that's me.

When I began wrestling my mind-set was: I gotta be me. Like me, hate me, I am just being me. For many of my formative years, I was not me. At least not the man I am today. It was a long rocky, winding, and fairly steep road to get where I am today (no, not stuck to my couch). I have experienced the good, the bad, the tough, the glad, and the sad; plenty of blood, sweat, tears . . . and any other tired old phrase you can think of.

But enough of the doom and gloom.

> In Orangeville, you have two choices: work in a factory in town, or, if you are really lucky, land a job in Toronto.

It all started in a sleepy little town named Orangeville, Ontario, in Canada. It was a nice town, a working-class town, located forty minutes northwest of Toronto. In Orangeville, you have two choices: work in a factory in town, or, if you are really lucky, land a job in Toronto. Even at a young age my goal was not to settle with picking between these choices, but to exceed them.

However, we need to go a little farther back, so let's cue the fuzzy dream sequence music and journey to a time when everyone's favorite Edgemeister was still kicking in his mom's stomach like Lars Ulrich of Metallica performing "One."

My mom, Judy Copeland, was born January 2, 1953. She left home at the age of seventeen. Eventually she got married and pregnant with yours truly. Before I was born this guy took off. Not exactly a class act. Bitter? In my teens, maybe there was a little bitterness. It's still something I don't bring up with my mom. Why, you ask? Partly because, at this point, I don't care. Also because I feel it may open old wounds. I have never met the man. In fact, I've never even seen his picture. Why would I want to meet someone like that? If anything, it taught me what *not* to do when I become a father. Besides, as I am about to explain, I never felt like I was missing anything growing up.

My mom.

I was born weighing in at 10 pounds 12 ounces at 7:05 A.M. on October 30, 1973, at the Orangeville Hospital. We picked up stakes after I was born and moved to nearby Cambridge, Ontario. By the time I was two we were back in Orangeville.

My mom was now twenty-three and I was three and we were back where we started, in illustrious Orangeville. It was tough but fun, at least for me. My mom worked two jobs, secretary during the day and waitress at night. (So tip well, because I know what waitresses go through.) When my mom headed to the waitressing job, I would either go to my grandparents' or one of my uncles would come over. Almost all of my mom's family lived in Orangeville. These were fun years. I would pretend to fall asleep on my grandparents' couch just so I could hear my grandmother say "Bless his little heart," and then she would kiss me on the head. I can still hear it like it was yesterday.

My grandparents had nine children, five boys and four girls. All the boys played hockey and all but one played goal. Let me just state that in order to play goal you need to have a screw loose (says the man who dives off fifteen-foot ladders). Being born in Canada, you are also born into hockey.

Outside at my grandparents'.

You see, this was the 1970s, and the Toronto Maple Leafs had some great players: Darryl Sittler (who I later played a yearly charity game with), Bjore Salming, Lanny MacDonald, and Mike Palmateer in goal. I would place my fat little butt on my grandpa's foot for his famous horse ride, surrounded by my uncles watching hockey on television. While all of this was going on, my mom was working. She would close down the restaurant, come get me around two A.M., and get up the next morning and do it all over again. To me, this was normal, and I was never lacking in the love department. I was always surrounded by loving family members.

Sometimes I would stay home and my uncles Randy and Gary would take on the babysitting duties. I was always close to Randy and Gary. In a way they became both father and brother figures even though

Gary was only nine years older than me. They were also the brothers who were closest to my mom. To me, they were the ultimate cool, second only to my new discovery: the hottest band in the land, KISS! They were

Me and my uncle Gary.

17

larger than life, they were characters. They had cool music but who cares, Ace Frehley was the spaceman and his guitar shot sparks! Gene Simmons spat blood and threw fiery swords! Wow! To my tiny three-year-old mind, this was it!

I grew up listening to music with my mom and uncles. My mom loved the Eagles, Led Zeppelin, America, and the Beatles. To this day I still love those bands. In my uncles' eyes, no band touched Queen, although Cheap Trick was close. I remember being enthralled by the album covers, studying them for hours while I listened to the music. Anytime I hear music from that era, it takes me back to those times.

However, for me, it was KISS. My mom understood that they were harmless, but Gary did not understand their appeal. Finally he relented, and asked to borrow my KISS Dynasty album for one of his parties. I had converted him to the KISS Army! I believe that KISS played a larger role in my childhood than even I realized. One night I scared the hell out of Randy. Let me set the scene: It was a dark and stormy night. The sky, she was angry that night, my friends, and the rain beat a tribal-like rhythm against the windows. Okay, I'm exaggerating, but you have to admit, it did sound pretty good. Anyway, this night Randy was babysitting me as I lay sound asleep on the couch (almost like a crowd watching an Al Snow match—sorry, Al, I had to throw in at least one). Meanwhile, Randy settled into a chair for a cozy night of "quality" seventies-era television. Little by little, he felt a strange presence. He turned his head to realize that the strange presence was me. I was on all fours right beside his face, on the arm of the couch. Did I forget to mention that my teeth were bared and I was growling? Now, before you start to think I'm Linda Blair from the *Exorcist,* hear me out. I was just dreaming that I was Peter Criss, the Cat Man, and drummer for KISS. That's my story and I'm stickin' to it! Suffice it to say, this threw Randy for a loop. At this point my mom walked in and saw what I was doing, and Randy took this opportunity to slowly creep out the front door.

My first dream was to become a rock star.

I would constantly run around with my little belly poking out of the bottom of my baby blue KISS Destroyer T-shirt. I had long, curly, platinum-blond hair (I refused a haircut even then), and my trusty red-and-white plastic guitar was placed firmly in hand. Essentially, you would have to say that my first dream was to become a rock star. Everyone around me wanted to play for the Leafs and wield a hockey stick. Not me, I wanted to wield a Les Paul guitar. Now, that's not to say that I didn't get my fair share of hockey, trust me, I did. I usually got plucked in between the pipes for my uncles shooting practice. I still don't understand that one, they were all goalies.

My other early childhood fixation was superheroes and comic books. Once again, my childhood obsession would rear its head in strange ways. One day, while my mom was in the kitchen, I decided in my infinite wisdom to do a back-flip off the coffee table. Hey, Spider-Man could do it, why not me? That question got answered quick, fast, and in a hurry. I landed squarely on my head, spraining my neck (this would become a recurring theme in my life). When my mom took me to the hospital, the doctor started to grill her about what happened. She told them I was in

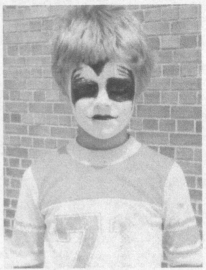

Now, you know what my favorite Halloween costume was.

the other room playing Batman. The look of doubt was still on their faces until I spoke up to say that I was playing Spider-Man, not Batman. I mean, duh! Spider-Man was way cooler than Batman.

Thankfully, for my mom's sake, my first day of kindergarten was quickly approaching. On that fateful, first day of school, my mom walked me right up to the sidewalk, tears in her eyes. I think she felt like she was throwing me in the deep end of the pool, hoping I wouldn't drown. To me it was no big deal, and besides, I wanted to know if anyone else liked KISS. (No one did.) It was around this time that I fell into my shy, reclusive stage (which seemed to last until I was fifteen). Around my mom and the rest of my family, I was me: fun-loving, outgoing Bam-Bam (one of my childhood nicknames). At school, I receded into the background. My grades were fine, but even if I knew the answer to a question, and the teacher looked my way, I would pretend to be tying my shoes. Maybe it's because I felt so safe and secure around my family that I shut down when they were not around. Who knows, maybe some child psychologist reading this can figure it out.

To this day my mom doesn't have her driver's license. I've offered cars, poked, pleaded, and prodded, but she will just not take the driving plunge. What this meant when I was younger was that it was one hell of a long walk to school. No bus route ran by our apartment, so we would throw on the boots and slush through the frigid Canadian winter. These grueling walks, though, were a blessing in disguise, because I met my very first best friend, Dwayne Harkness. Dwayne and his mom walked the same route as us, and soon we became inseparable. We may not have been the coolest kids, but we had each other. We actually lived a good distance apart, but we had our meeting point on our way to Princess Elizabeth Public School (home of the Pythons, although the name has been changed to the Pandas, which must surely strike fear into every opponents' heart). Because we lived so far apart, Dwayne and I could only hang out together at school and on weekends. Weekdays were a write-off. Although not a social butterfly, I was able to make another best friend, right across the street from me, Rob Moody. We lived on Broadway. This might make you think bright lights and big cities, but sorry to disappoint, it did not live up to that legendary name. Looking back now, I would have to say that our apartment . . . sucked, for lack of a better term. We were not exactly affluent, but my mom did her best, busting her hump at two jobs. It got tough, but I was still too young to understand the hardship my mom was going through. To me, walking everywhere, having a little two-coil furnace for heat, no phone, and seeing my breath in bed at night was no big deal (now, however, my big crybaby ass could not handle it).

> Looking back now, I would have to say that our apartment . . . sucked, for lack of a better term.

Across the street, life for Rob was very similar, so we clicked. We hung out in the back alleys behind our apartment buildings, doing everything. Street hockey, skateboarding, G.I. Joe, you name it. It may not sound like all that much fun, but somehow it was. We didn't know any better.

Thanks to Dwayne and Rob I was able to get through those first few years of school. It was nice to have someone to lean on. Occasionally, I still keep in touch with Dwayne. Sadly, I have fallen out of touch with Rob. Last I heard he was somewhere in northern Ontario. If you're reading this, "Hi, Rob."

t was not until later that I noticed we had a lot less materially than other people. I had friends I would visit after school with nice, big houses. From there I would come home, navigate my way up rickety old stairs from the back alley to our apartment. This was not your typical apartment building. There were only three apartments. And for some reason our bathroom had a second door that opened onto the building's hallway, which the building's other occupants used to get to their apartments. Strange setup.

We also didn't have a shower. Instead, we had an old claw-foot bathtub. Looking back, there were quite a few classic elements in that apartment, which, with the proper money, could have been nice. We, however, did not have the proper money floating around. We struggled to make the rent. Sometimes I'm sure we got behind on the rent so I could eat, but my mom always struggled on. She was too stubborn to give in (I know where I got that trait from).

When I started to pay attention to the disparities in my life—comparing my life to that of some of my friends—I started to question my mom. Somehow I always got the KISS action figure for Christmas or the Sherwood goalie stick for my

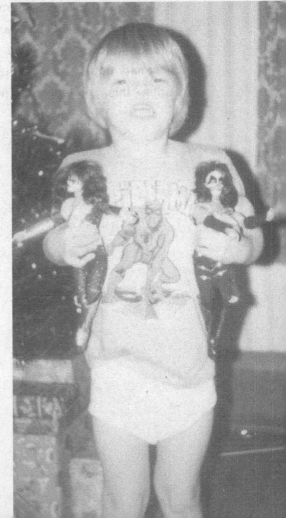

The happiest kid
in all of Orangeville.

birthday, but I still wondered why Santa brought the "rich kids" more. Imagine, as a single mom, busting your butt as a secretary and a waitress, trying to answer that one. I even remember saying, "I wish I lived somewhere else." God how that must have made her feel, and to this day I still kick myself for spitting that ball of hate out.

Somehow, in my little mind, I believed that kids who lived in houses were somehow better than me.

Somehow, in my little mind, I believed that kids who lived in houses were somehow better than me. Maybe that's where my shyness came from. It's amazing the things that seem important when you're a little kid. It got to a point where I would sprint down the back alley to the old stairs, just so no one would see where I lived (like anyone was watching, or cared). It was stupid of me, and I know it hurt my mom's feelings (sorry, Ma). She tried hard to make ends meet and make me a good person. Thankfully, the lesson took (I think). Like I mentioned before, when it comes to love, I was never lacking. She was able to provide me with Spider-Man, KISS, and food on the table, just not the lavish house that the other kids had. In a strange way, I think it actually helped to form the man writing this, and taught me not to take anything for granted.

Me and Gary.

I t was on May 19, 1982, that my family was rocked by disaster. My uncle Gary, who was only seventeen, was gravely injured in an auto accident. He was nine years older than me and he was like the brother I never had. My uncles Randy and Joe were also like father figures. It shook me to my very core. I could not fully grasp what was happening.

I remember going to my grandparents' apartment in the middle of the night. The accident happened in Owen Sound, Ontario, at around one A.M. Gary and four of his friends were on their way home after a

25

My uncle Gary at 15.
I still miss him.

lacrosse game. It was late, the roads were wet, and they were young. Gary was thrown from the car and was in a coma. From that night, and for the next six days, I was at Toronto General Hospital, crying. Finally, on May 26, the decision was made to take Gary off life support.

I was young, but I could still comprehend that this was just not right. He was like my brother, one of my best friends, my soccer coach that coming summer, on his way to the Edmonton Oilers farm team and possibly an NHL career. I just kept asking myself, Why? I still don't have an answer, but I gotta believe that someone that good, went someplace better. At the funeral, my grandmother remembered hearing my voice reciting the Lord's Prayer louder than anyone else. That prayer just seemed important to me. My mom remembers me clutching her hand. She thought I was trying to support her. I know she supported me, so I guess we supported each other. It's a blow I don't think my family will ever recover from.

Now there was a gaping hole in our lives. I could never replace Gary, but that was when something appeared on my radar screen to help fill the void. I floated around for a long time until one day my TV screen was filled by a platinum blond, yellow-and-red-clad behemoth with a definite fire burning in his eyes. He was telling me to drink my milk, say my prayers, and take my vitamins.

That behemoth was Hulk Hogan.

I floated around for a long time until one day my TV screen was filled by a platinum blond, yellow-and-red-clad behemoth with a definite fire burning in his eyes.

Wrestling had sunk its teeth into me, and I was hooked in quicker than a Chris Benoit crossface. I have to admit, as I sat in my old rocking chair, my feet next to the coil heater, Hulk Hogan had me. He made me feel like I could accomplish anything I put my mind to. As cheesy as that sounds, like Kurt Angle would say, "It's damn true!" I sat glued to the tube. I watched them all: *Superstars, Wrestling Challenge, Wrestling Spotlight,* and *Maple Leaf Wrestling,* which featured host Billy Red Lyons and his mantra of "Don't cha dare miss it." Well, Billy Red (God rest his soul), I did not miss it. I ate wrestling up quicker than Big Show at an all-you-can-eat buffet. Once a month was *Saturday Night's Main Event.*

Here I am lifting Jay (those are his feet dangling on the left).

27

Picture a vampire sucking the TV for all of the wrestling it had, until it was bled dry. I was Count Freakin' Dracula.

My mom and I would sit down with potato chips and popcorn, and I'd quickly be swept away into my own world. I would not hear any questions that my mom would ask. I was the definition of tunnel vision. Picture a vampire sucking the TV for all of the wrestling it had, until it was bled dry. I was Count Freakin' Dracula.

International Wrestling from Montreal featured Rick Martel, Tom Zenk, Sadistic Steve DiSalvo, Eddie "The Brain" Creatchman, his son, "Pretty Boy" Floyd Creatchman, "Mr. Perpetual Motion" (quite possibly the worst wrestling moniker ever), and a man who would someday help to get my wrestling career off the ground, Sweet Daddy Siki (more on him later).

BC All Star Wrestling was on after World Wrestling Federation and paled in comparison. Actually, it sucked and blew at the same time, but I still watched. They had one diamond in the rough, appropriately named "Diamond" Timothy Flowers. Flowers would always curbstomp the Frog (a name possibly worse than Mr. Perpetual Motion, and yes, the Frog looked about as fearsome as he sounded).

From Calgary came *Stampede Wrestling,* which invaded my senses. It was like an incoming missile on my wrestling radar screen. Bret Hart, Davey Boy Smith, Dynamite Kid, and Bad News Allen all in the beginning of their careers. Eventually I watched in awe as Owen Hart, Chris Benoit, Jushin Liger, Hiroshi Hase, and Brian Pillman all started their careers under Stu Hart's legendary Stampede banner. This was a completely different hybrid, greatly influenced by the Japanese and English wrestling styles. They had Ladder matches! What? That's right, Bret vs. Bad News in a Ladder match before Ladder matches were famous (or infamous, depending on your point of view). For me, it was unheard of. (Little did I know the part ladders would play in my future.) The host of *Stampede Wrestling* was Ed Whalen. At the end of every show he would hit his tag line, "In the meantime, and in between time, that's it, another edition of *Stampede Wrestling.* Bye bye now." I would recite it in unison with him every week. He created so many great terms like "The ol' malfunction at the junction," which he used for any big bump.

Every week Ed would also host *Pro Wrestling Plus.* This program showcased wrestling from around the world. Wrestlers from the NWA,

Continental, Mid-South, Puerto Rico, and Mid-Atlantic regions would be represented on this show. Guys I could only read about in the pages of *Pro Wrestling Illustrated,* like Ric Flair, Jerry Lawler, Dr. Tom Prichard, Austin Idol, the Von Erichs, Bruiser Brody, and Carlos Colon were highlighted on *Pro Wrestling Plus.* I could not get enough, but they only played thirty-second clips of the matches. We could not afford a VCR, so I was left with quick images and pictures in my mind.

Around this time TSN (Total Sports Network) picked up AWA Wrestling and broadcasted it to Canada. Rick Martel was their World Champion. Guys like Stan Hansen, Larry "The Axe" Hennig, his son Curt Hennig, Nick Bockwinkel, Larry Zbysko, and the Midnight Rockers—Shawn Michaels and Marty Jannetty—all busted heads there. Even Hulk Hogan had worked there before he jumped ship to the bright lights of New York City and World Wrestling Federation.

Through all this wrestling fanaticism, my mom would sit beside me. She would humor me and calm me down when King Kong Bundy would attack Hogan or Randy Savage would do the same to Ricky Steamboat. We would buy all the new wrestling action figures (the classic rubber ones), and when I said I wanted to be a wrestler, she would always respond with a Tony the Tiger–like

> When I said I wanted to be a wrestler, she would always respond with a Tony the Tiger–like "Grreeaat!"

"Grreeaat!" (It was actually more of a "Go for it," but I couldn't think of a cereal mascot with that catchphrase.) She probably didn't want to discourage me at such a young age. My excitement with wrestling was infectious, and I think she secretly enjoyed it as much as I did.

One day, my mom and my uncle Randy surprised me with tickets for the World Wrestling Federation at Maple Leaf Gardens. Better yet, the seats were in the fourth row ringside! I don't know how they did it, but they pulled it off. It was my mom, Randy, my soon to be Aunt Sandy, and me. I will never forget the butterflies I had walking up to that classic old building. Somehow we got lucky and were able to stand at the entrance where the wrestlers entered the building. They were all passing me, George "The Animal" Steele, Tito Santana, Hillbilly Jim, and King Kong Bundy. They were massive, giants, walking towers. I was in awe.

By the time Parisi hit his Cannonball, I was hooked for life.

At Maple Leaf Gardens with Jay. Look at those "Pythons."

Maple Leaf Gardens had a famous black rampway that led down to the ring. I had watched everyone walk that ramp on *Maple Leaf Wrestling*, and now I was there. The first match—my first live match—was Rene Goulet vs. Tony "Cannonball" Parisi. Admittedly, neither guy really captured my imagination. But by the time Parisi hit his Cannonball, I was hooked for life. The main event that night was Jesse "the Body" Ventura and "Macho Man" Randy Savage vs. Tito Santana and the Junkyard Dog. Of course, I cheered for all the babyfaces, although at that time they were just the good guys to me. In my eyes they stood for what was right. Wrestling was very black and white in those days. There were no shades of gray, it was cut and dry. With all of that being said, I could not help but like the Macho Man and Ventura; I just wouldn't admit it.

Another thing that I would never admit was the claim that wrestling was predetermined, or worse yet, the dreaded word (drum roll please) fake! Little did I know that I would later come to understand, first-hand, that wrestling was indeed predetermined, but it was definitely not fake (the metal plate in my neck attests to that).

It seemed like I was not the only one to have discovered wrestling. *WrestleMania* was happening, and the popularity was exploding. It just so happens that around this time another kid (one month younger, to be exact), named Jason Reso, had stumbled upon wrestling in the neighboring town (actually more like a hamlet) of Grand Valley. That kid Jason would end up being my "brother" Christian (sorry to disappoint, we're not really brothers). We'll get to him soon.

About this time that kid Jason Reso moved to Orangeville and started attending Princess Elizabeth. He had that mysterious new-guy quality. I was willing to look past the fact that he wore huge tennis wristbands, because he had a ninja star! Ninjas couldn't hold a candle to wrestlers, but it would have still been a hell of a fight in my eyes. Despite the ninja star, wrestling was number one in Jay's book, too. He had discovered wrestling a year before, when he had broken his arm and had nothing to do but watch TV. I'm sure the wrestling gods must have been smiling the day that we met. Eventually Jay and I became inseparable as well as outcasts at school. For some reason we were the only two not invited to parties. It was probably because we were (and currently are) huge geeks. That was fine with us; we had wrestling.

Even with my wrestling obsession, I found the time to experience my first real kiss. I had been "going steady" with a little redhead named Cindy Crockford. Cindy was born on the same day as me, in the same hospital. I was the only boy in the maternity ward that day. You might think this was a sign of studliness to come. You would be horribly wrong, as you are about to see. Anyway, I was in Grade 6 and dating Cindy. I had walked her home and suddenly realized that she was looking up at me, expecting a kiss. Okay, here goes. I closed my eyes and took the plunge with my mouth closed, expecting a peck on the lips. Cindy was obviously a little more experienced at the whole kissing thing, because she had her mouth opened wide. I didn't realize in time and completely botched my first kiss worse than Jonathan Coachman trying to wrestle a match. Unlike Coach, I quickly recovered and salvaged the kiss.

Although I had a girlfriend, Jay and I were still attached at the hip. One day, during our outcast, rebels-

Did I mention that we were really cool?

without-a-clue phase, we decided to pull an all-nighter. Oh yeah, we were going to prove how cool we were by staying out all night, thinking we would have a great story to tell. Jay told his parents that he was crashing at my place and I told my mom that I would be staying at Jay's. So, at eleven that night, we found ourselves hanging out at St. Andrew's Catholic School . . . by ourselves. Real cool. Of course, we had nothing to do, but we were committed by now. Maybe we should have *been* committed. About this time, it started lightning, quickly followed by a storm. Did I mention that we were really cool? We walked across town until we finally gave in, found a cardboard box, set it up in an alley, and slept there. Believe it or not, the rain beating down on the box put me to sleep. Around seven the next morning, we woke up and walked to Jay's house, where we hid in the garage until his parents were up and it seemed like a believable time for us to be walking home from my house. Like I said, rebel without a clue and not exactly Fonzarelli cool.

Like I said, rebel without a clue and not exactly Fonzarelli cool.

Very occasionally, small independent wrestling shows would roll— actually more like limp—into the Orangeville Arena. Jay and I started our wrestling networking at an early age. Somehow we met the local promoter and started helping out. We put up posters, set up chairs, and the ultimate: helped to set up the ring! The promoter would even let us get in and roll around the ring for a little while (the ring I would eventually have my first match in). Jay took this opportunity to scale the ropes and pounce on his brother Josh, creaming him with the best high cross body block I have ever seen to this day. That ended our fun, especially Josh's. He felt the effects for about a week. Once, we took a chance and jumped in the ring during intermission. Now, I would never advise doing this during a WWE show, because security, or one of us, would take your head off, but that night Jay and I caught eyes and rolled into the ring. Obviously, the local security did not care because Jay hit me with a clothesline and I had time to hit him with a Macho Man–like axe handle, without the height and grace. We then hightailed it out of the ring like the Roadrunner and Speedy Gonzales, or better yet Superman and Flash, but before we did, a magical thing happened. We actually garnered a reaction. A reaction that we, of course, turned into epic proportions rivaling that of our beloved Hulkster himself. Suffice to say, the wrestling bug bit even deeper.

A magical thing happened. We actually garnered a reaction . . . The wrestling bug bit even deeper.

On these smaller shows you had Sweet Daddy Siki (once again),

At the Orangeville Arena with Paul Diamond and Jay.

Tony Atlas, Vic Steamboat, Abdullah the Butcher, Tracey Smothers, Paul Diamond, Crazy Chris Colt, the Cream Team (once again a B-R-utal name), Chris Evans, and a man who scared me half to death and had me running from my seat like a little schoolgirl, The Original Sheik. It was great to be so close to the action, but a disappointment to head back to the doldrums of school on Monday.

The Getalong Gang without Jay—
me (full mullet), Fatty, Johnny, and John.

The time had finally come. After being shunned for the last two years of public school, it was time to move on and become shunned in high school. Of course, high school, and everyone there, intimidated me. I was a loner and an introvert, and high school added fuel to that fire. I was tall, skinny, and sporting a fully intact mullet. Cut me some slack, at this point mullets were cool (how they ever got to be that way is still beyond me). Jay was still my only real friend and our lives revolved around wrestling and skateboarding.

While still in the very awkward and intimidating Grade 9, I became a target for a band of bullies. They decided to make my early teen years a living hell (at least that's the way it felt at the time). This next scene could have been used in any high school teen flick. Unfortunately, it happened to me.

One day while standing at my locker, I turned around to find myself surrounded. I was thrown up against my locker and punched square in the chin. Up until that point I had never been in what could be classified as a real fight. And that didn't change this day. There were three of them and just one little ol' me.

Jay was at the other end of the school and I had no one to watch my back. So what did I do? Absolutely nothing. I stood there with a horrible feeling in the pit of my stomach, humiliated, in the middle of a packed hallway. That day I told myself I would never feel that way again. And I haven't.

In a strange way, this incident, along with everything that had happened before, motivated me. It motivated me to get to the gym. It motivated me to break out of my shell a little more. Most important, it pushed me toward my goal of becoming a wrestler. I know, it sounds like some

> I was tall, skinny, and sporting a fully intact mullet.

kind of motivational speech or a Tony Robbins infomercial, but that's what it took for me to wake up and grit my teeth. Now, don't get me wrong, I still wasn't exactly Rocky Balboa training in a Russian farmhouse for a fight with Ivan Drago, but it did light a fire under my narrow ass.

Thankfully fate worked with me, as it would so many times in the future. Going into Grade 10, I hit a growth spurt and gained weight. Puberty was good to me. I shot from five-nine to six-two and, along with Jay, joined the Orangeville Boxing Club. Not so coincidentally those bullies stopped bothering me—funny how these things work out. Eventually I hit a wall in my boxing training. My coaches wanted me to keep my weight at one hundred sixty pounds while standing six-two. This would have given me a huge reach advantage over most of my weight class, but it would also have me resembling a tree. Wrestling was already calling my name, so I politely said good-bye and hit the gym. Little by little my proportions grew to six-four and two hundred pounds.

I still felt like a scarecrow, but I was on my way. Jay joined me at the gym, where we firmly cemented prior friendships with Nick Cvjetkovich, John Posavac, and Johnny Newton. We had been friends for a while, and at the gym and at school we became affectionately known as the Getalong Gang. Nick's dad, Mike, owned the gym, the Orangeville Squash and Fitness Center. Our routine became training every day. If there was a World Wrestling Federation match on Pay-Per-View satellite, we would close the gym, watch it, and then head to the karate dojo downstairs to beat the hell out of one another.

The gym was on the outskirts of town but I would walk to it every day. One hour there, work out, one hour back, and trust me, sweat and Canadian winters do not mix. Luckily my Walkman (Discmans were still a rarity) helped the time go by. Sometimes I would get lucky and John would land his mom's old Dodge Aspen to come and get me. When Jay first got his license he picked me up in his parents' van to go hit the gym. The Resos had a sporting goods store, so the van was used for store purposes. By this time my mom and I had moved to a nicer apartment, and Jay had to circle behind the back of the building. Just as I said "Be careful, it's a tight squeeze," CRUNCH, the side of the van hit the corner of the building. Immediately beads of sweat emerged on his forehead. Jay's dad, Randy, is a tough, firm, but fair dude. He's real thick from power lifting in his younger days, so Jay was petrified.

The Resos are a great family and let Jay off pretty easy, but what a start to a driving career. Trust me, he has not improved much over the years.

During high school I also played baseball, soccer, volleyball, and basketball. We did not have a football team—let's face it, nothing can replace hockey in Canada. Once again I felt forced into quitting another sport. This time it was basketball, and it was not from any ultimatum to keep my weight down. Oh no, this time the ultimatum was cut my hair or quit the team. I did not see how my hair affected my game—just ask Steve Nash or Dirk Nowitski—so I quit. I knew wrestling was for me, and let's face it, I did not have Vince Carter's hops.

While all of this was happening, Jay and I would hit all the shows at Maple Leaf Gardens, the MLG. One day we lucked into seats right beside the ring. We burned those seat numbers into our memory and every other month we would call to get them. My mom and I didn't have a credit card, so Jay's mom would put the tickets on her card, and I would eventually pay her back (I think I'm all paid up, let me know, Carol).

They had gotten rid of the classic MLG rampway, but that just meant we could shake hands with the wrestlers. We knew where the wrestlers left the building, so it was time to strike up conversations. We were always very polite, but usually got brushed off until Bryan Adams and Barry Darsow, better known as Demolition, actually talked to us (who knew we would surpass their four tag title wins). I always try to remember that, especially with the position I'm in now. (We've told Bryan that story, which made him feel old, but it made me realize how to treat the fans. Bryan now lives down the road from me and he's still a class act. It's amazing how things can work out.)

That day taught me how <u>not</u> to treat a fan.

The opposite side of that fan-friendly spectrum was Tony Atlas, whom we had met several times at the local Orangeville shows. He was now back with World Wrestling Federation as Saba Simba. We saw him before an MLG show and called out "Hi, Tony!" We had spent enough time with him to garner a wave or a hello. Not Atlas, or should I say Simba. He completely ignored us. He was in no rush; he was just standing in the hallway by himself, but nothing. That day taught me how *not* to treat a fan. Thanks for something, Tony.

Most Likely To…

Win the WWE championship belt:
Adam Copeland and **Mike Whaley**

CHAPTER

This chapter of my life had some pleasant surprises. The *Toronto Star* supplied the first one. One week, Norm DaCosta's wrestling column had a trivia question. The prize was two free front-row tickets to the next World Wrestling Federation show at Copps Coliseum in Hamilton, Ontario. One day after school, while hanging out at Jay's, a phone call came. Little by little Jay's excitement level rose until he jumped off the phone and onto me, planting a big wet one on my cheek! Now, at this point, I had never had a serious girlfriend, but I knew which way I was inclined, so I was in complete shock. It ends up that the call was from the *Toronto Star* informing Jay that he had won the free tickets. We were in heaven, so I let the kiss slide.

We witnessed so many shows in that building throughout the years. The first ever *King of the Ring,* Flair vs. Hogan, Hart vs. Martel, Hennig vs. Taylor, and so many more. Who could foresee that, many years later, my first World Wrestling Federation match would take place there.

When it came to wrestling shows, I was pretty lucky. I ended up going to the famous Hulk Hogan vs. Paul "Mr. Wonderful" Orndoff match at Toronto's CNE Stadium. Sixty-five thousand other people also lucked out at going to that show.

During this time I received the ultimate surprise (pun intended). My mom somehow pooled together the resources to buy two tickets, eleventh row ringside, for *WrestleMania VI* at Toronto's SkyDome. This was the ultimate dream because I was on my way to the Ultimate Challenge. Hulk Hogan vs. The Ultimate Warrior. It also didn't hurt that The Hart Foundation, The Rockers, and Mr. Perfect were on the bill as well. They had quickly become my favorites.

The view from my seat at WrestleMania VI.

I had never felt electricity like the SkyDome that night.

I had never felt electricity like the SkyDome that night. The nearly 68,000 fans were split between Hulka-maniacs and Warrior fans. It was simply awesome (even though Hulk lost). This was my dream.

My mom had continued to see that look in my eyes. The look that appeared anytime I was around wrestling. I think she was starting to truly believe that I might do this for a living. Wrestling was not going away, and even if the popularity dwindled, I was still there, live or glued to the tube. There is no way I can truly convey the passion I had, and still have, for this business, although my mom can probably vouch for it.

Everyone at school knew I was a wrestling fanatic. In the yearbook I was voted most likely to become World Wrestling Federation champion (a prophecy I still need to make come true). Slowly but surely I was beginning to gain confidence. I had my good, tight, circle of friends (which has stayed intact to this day). We watched wrestling, listened to music, and worked out. Don't get me wrong, like any teenager, girls were definitely a priority, however that was the one place I was still lacking confidence. Looking back, I think I was a pretty well adjusted kid during my high school years. I tried smoking once, hated it, and have not touched a cigarette since. I had my first drunken binge at the age of sixteen—definitely not proud of that one—but my mom's reaction quickly snapped me out of my drunken stupor.

I tried smoking once, hated it, and have not touched a cigarette since.

She said she was disappointed, and that affected me more than any yelling fit could have. I never had another drink until I was of legal age, and only sporadically after that. To each their own, it's just not for me.

She said she was disappointed, and that affected me more than any yelling fit could have.

I was working after school now so I could help out with the ever-increasing grocery bill. My place of employment was the Orangeville Raceway, a horse track. I sat in a little wooden booth (with no heat) and took money in exchange for parking tickets. I was making $3.25 an hour and freezing my ass off, so I devised a moneymaking scheme. I would avoid handing out a ticket every tenth car and pocket the two dollars. There's not much to do in Orangeville, so quite a few cars came through.

Eventually I saved enough money to purchase my first car, a 1981 Mercury Cougar. My days of walking to school in minus-forty-degree-Celsius weather were over. No more walking to the gym. Our days of wrestling in snowbanks from one side of town to the other were over. Or so I thought: Car insurance slapped me back to reality. I never counted on how much it would cost. My mom did not drive and I was young, with no driving experience. Somehow I did not see myself coming up with $4,000, so I paid my initial deposit, got my sticker and stopped paying. Then I drove with no insurance. I drove as little as possible, but I still did it. I wouldn't advise doing this, it's not worth the stress, and it's hard to drive with your fingers and toes crossed.

CHAPTER

Now I was in Grade 11 with my friend Nick, who was also in my French class. I took French for eleven years and all I can do is count to ten (une, deux, trois, quatre, cinq . . . . okay, it's only to five, leave me alone!). Obviously, I was not paying much attention. Nick and I had always been comic book geeks, and very artistic, so we spent our time doodling. We would create and draw our own characters and proceed to book a wrestling show. On our spares (free periods) we would all gather in a remote "squared circle" near the library of the school, and "wrestle" these matches. Yes, like I said, we were geeks, but we were having fun. Nick was Decker Hard or the original Sexton Hardcastle. Jay was Sweet Daddy Freak-out. John Posavac was the One Man Posse-Vac. I was the Blonde Bomber . . . Splint (brutal, I know). We had others, like Vicious Virgil Van Eat Me, the Barncat Keith Brown, and Canadian Cornflake (don't ask me why). We had everyone not involved in the match sitting on a picnic table announcing. The two "combatants" would very gingerly wrestle around. We definitely knew it was easy to get hurt, so we were careful.

For some reason, around this time I started to gain a reputation as a "tough guy" around school. Because of this, some guy named Jake Vivian, who was already out of high school, decided he wanted to fight me. Being a teenager, my testosterone was flying high, so I said sure, why not? I had no beef with the guy, but he obviously had one with me. I found out later that he wanted to pad his reputation by beating my ass. That didn't work out too well for him. It took place in "the catwalk" off-school property. John was with me and we walked out the back doors to see the catwalk surrounded, with Jake standing in the middle trying to pull off his best Jean-Claude Van Damme impersonation. I entered the circle and it quickly closed behind me. It opened about thirty seconds later with Jake lying facedown, licking his wounds. Now, I'm not claiming to be Ali, and I'm not condoning fighting, but sometimes you just have to do it. I didn't have to fight again until my bouncing days, but that was still to come.

My wrestling fixation had not abated, and pretty soon it would pay off, with the *Toronto Star* coming back into my life. This time it was not free tickets, it was free wrestling training and a possible ticket to my dream. The *Star* had a wrestling column every week that I read religiously. One week I read the magic words "If you've dreamed of being a wrestler here's your chance!" That got my attention, and I read on. All I had to do was write an essay detailing why I wanted to be a wrestler. The prize: free wrestling training! I put pen to paper right away trying to detail why I should be the person to win the prize. I wrote and rewrote. I lost count of all the drafts, but finally I was satisfied. I tried to keep a level head to avoid embarrassing myself, which, in

the end, I think I avoided. The essays were mailed to Sully's Gym, located in Parkdale, a pretty rough neighborhood in Toronto, where the winner would be trained for the ring wars by Sweet Daddy Siki and Ron Hutchinson.

Jay vowed that he, too, would write an essay, but eventually backed out and postponed his wrestling training for another two and a half years. He's still never explained that one. Now, I don't want to get too deep on my Edgeheads here, but my mentality was, and is, if you're afraid to go out on a limb, how can you get the fruit?

My soon-to-be trainer, Sweet Daddy Siki.

Of course, as soon as that essay was out of my hands, I was anxiously awaiting the result, ready to grab that fruit. My mind was consumed and I needed something to ease my tension. Thankfully, like he's done so many times over the years, my good buddy Nick saved the day with the perfect idea, at the perfect time.

CHAPTER

For no reason in particular, Nick, Jay, and I have always referred to each other as Fatty, Fat Kid, and Fatso, respectively. So for the remainder of this book, because he can never trump me on this now that it's in print, Nick will be forever immortalized as Fatty.

One day while stressing out about the essay contest, my mom entered my room and said, "Fatty's on the phone." (Yep, my mom refers to Nick as Fatty, too.) When I had the phone to my ear Fatty hit me with the idea that would help my frazzled nerves. "Let's go to Fort Lauderdale for spring break," bellowed the Fat One. I thought about it for all of a nanosecond and replied, "Let's do it." I had saved some more money from work and decided that this would be a good way to spend some of it.

Fatty, Ken Dorie, and I crammed ourselves into Chevrolet's version of a sardine can, the Sprint. This was my first road experience and I was ready, armed with my Metallica, Faith No More, and Red Hot Chili Peppers cassettes. Detroit, Cincinnati, Atlanta—all of these cities rolling by was pretty mind-boggling to a kid who had never been outside Ontario.

We were making good time, considering the Sprint's limited abilities, until we hit Macon, Georgia, at three A.M. We got pulled over, for of all things speeding. Personally, I don't think it was possible to speed in the Sprint, but Macon's supposed finest claimed we were. After adding a seat belt fine and a ticket for failing to signal, the grand total came to $300. After nailing us in the solar plexus with that news, they told us that we would have to come down to the station. I had only heard that line in movies and it always meant bad news, so I braced myself for the worst.

When I got to the station I realized that I had more teeth than the whole force, and immediately scenes from the movie *Deliverance*

flashed through my head. They took Fatty into the back and left Ken and me up front to ponder our fate. About an hour later the police informed us that we had a pretty mouthy friend. Once it sunk in that they hadn't said my friend had a pretty mouth, I was able to hear that Fatty needed to pay the fine now, or spend some good ol' fashioned jail time until he did.

This would prove to be a problem. You see, Fatty had supplied the car, and we would be staying at his grandparents' condo complex so we brought the money. This meant that Nick had roughly $20 to his name. Ken and I had $150 each and forked it over to get the fat ass out. We quickly got the hell out of Macon with $20 in our pockets. We'd been screwed like a hooker in heat, but we were on our way. The Sprint managed to float into Fort Lauderdale on fumes and we looked as shell-shocked as the crowd who witnessed the Kennel from Hell match.

We'd been screwed like a hooker in heat, but we were on our way.

There is a reason why I mention this trip, and that is because it was monumental, at least for me. Was it the defining moment when I became a man? Hell no! Was it the occasion when I lost my virginity at age seventeen to a petite twenty-one-year-old blonde in a purple thong bikini? Hell yes, and about damn time!

Was it the defining moment when I became a man? Hell no!

Obviously this ended up being a great trip, but unfortunately we had to head back up to Canada and the stress of the essay contest. We had another twenty-four-hour drive filled with fast food, some money (thanks to Nick's grandmother), Nirvana, Tom Petty, Metallica, Ugly Kid Joe (remember them?), and great memories.

CHAPTER

We were back in Canada and I decided to commemorate my momentous spring break and the plucking of my virginity by getting a tattoo. Yeah, I know it doesn't make much sense, but we had all decided to get one. John got a rose. Nick got a rose, and became addicted to tattoos. Johnny got some kind of weird leprechaun. Jay got a bulldog with a yellow rose in its mouth. Fatty designed my tattoo. Jay and I wanted similar ink so we designed a shark hitting a most muscular pose similar to Jay's bulldog. At the time I thought it was pretty cool. I was wrong, and a cartoon called the Street Sharks emphasized that point. They looked identical to my tattoo, which Triple H constantly reminded me of (the bastard!).

I was still firmly entrenched in my little unheated wooden shack at the Orangeville Raceway. I was unfazed, though, because in my mind the winds of change were blowing for young Adam Copeland. I assumed that the loss of my virginity would be the beginning of a hot streak that even the 1972 Miami Dolphins couldn't touch. Strangely enough, I was not that far off. Two weeks after my spring fling, I received the phone call that would change my life forever. The very distinctive

In the ring at Sully's.

Texas drawl of Sweet Daddy Siki was on the line, and he wanted me to come to Sully's Gym so he and Ron Hutchison could take a look at me. Okay, I thought, this *had* to be a good sign.

By now I had run my Cougar into the ground, so my grandpa, mom,

We went inside and were hit with the distinct smell of jockstraps and mildew.

and I piled into my grandpa's car and off we went. We pulled up to a dilapidated old building straight out of *Rocky*. I almost expected to see Stallone stroll by, bouncing his squash ball. We went inside and were hit with the distinct smell of jockstraps and mildew. It may have reeked, but it reeked of character. It was in worse shape than any apartment my mom and I had ever lived in, but I loved it. We walked up two very unsafe looking flights of stairs and entered Sully's.

In the corner of a large room filled with boxing equipment was the ring. It was actually a boxing ring that doubled as a wrestling ring on weekends. There were several students doing their thing, which fascinated me, but I was called into the office, where Siki and Ron were waiting.

Little did I know that I was about to enter the final stage of the contest. Ron and Siki told me to have a seat and proceeded to hurl horror stories at me to really test my ambition.

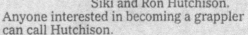

The WCW is upset over this and wants Luger to stay away from doing any promotional work until next March.

And the winner is: Adam Copeland of Orangeville, 18, won the wrestling essay contest conducted by Sully's Gym.

The 224-pound Copeland will be taught professional wrestling by Sweet Daddy Siki and Ron Hutchison. Anyone interested in becoming a grappler can call Hutchison.

Copeland

Madusa-Gilbert split: Madusa Macelli and Eddie Gilbert, who got married less than three months ago, have split. A new angle on television has the Dangerous Alliance claiming Ricky Steamboat is in love with Madusa.

Being an African-American wrestler in the sixties (with a blond Afro), Siki had experienced some tough times. He ate out of Dumpsters, slept in alleys, and made no money. He said that could all happen to me unless I really wanted it. Oh, how I wanted it! It was the final test, and I passed it! They let me sweat for a week, but I won the contest! Free training! The training otherwise would have cost $3,000. For a single-parent household that would not be a possibility, so winning the contest was a godsend. Thanks to Ron and Siki, I was on my way.

Wrestling class took place every Saturday and Sunday, and it was amazing. I quickly realized that watching wrestling doesn't translate to being a blue-chipper in the ring. My preying mantis–like form was awkward, but I was persistent. We really got put through our paces, and that was before we ever stepped foot in the ring. An hour of stairs, bulling (locking up; struggle back and forth), laps of the stadium, and a daily torture routine called the PTA—a very appropriate acronym of pain,

My class at Sully's. What a motley-looking crew.

We really got put through our paces . . . a daily torture routine called the PTA—a very appropriate acronym of pain, torture, and agony.

torture, and agony. We ached through thirty minutes of the PTA every workout. Ron and Siki would shout orders: drop to your back, stomach, up stomach, push-ups, up, back and so on and so on. It was tough but it built up what I call my wrestling callus. Depending on Ron's mood, PTA sometimes took place on the hardwood floor. There were times I was sure we would go through and end up in a crumpled heap on the first floor. Luckily, we never did.

After this we very slowly made our way to the ring for an hour's worth of real pain. Ron and Siki were sticklers for the basics. At the time it was frustrating, but in the long run it paid off. We had a good group of guys. The standouts were Keith Assoun (Zakk Wyld) and Joe Hitchen (Joe E. Legend). Although they'd been at the school for a full year before me, they quickly accepted me into their inner circle of two. The class slowly grew as Joe Dorgan (Johnny Swinger) and Rob Etcheverria (El Fuego) joined. Now there was more talent, ideas, and styles for all of us to play off. The only limiting factor was the ring itself. It doubled as a boxing ring during the week, but would have been more useful as a cinder block. The damn thing was bulletproof, a squared circle forged from steel. It was also very tiny, measuring twelve by fourteen. By comparison, WWE rings are twenty by twenty. The ceiling was very low, with multiple pipes hanging down, which killed my head on a leapfrog. This small monstrosity was built into a corner, so that meant we hurtled into a wall on two sides of the ring. I loved every inch of it.

The ring was built into a corner, so that meant we hurtled into a wall on two sides . . . I loved every inch of it.

My first match. I'm the one in the Zubaz.

A collapsed lung! I was sure of it. Every breath was a struggle. The smirking faces at the edge of my vision were blurry. Death was upon me and he held his sickle high! I had just taken my very first vertical suplex. I had sucked in enough air to force out, "I'm okay, let's do it again." In case you have not realized it yet, here is a news flash: I am extremely stubborn and about as sharp as a bowling ball. Hitting the ropes left green bruises on my side. My elbows had turned a strange shade of yellow. I may have resembled a bruised banana, but I was undeterred.

Death was upon me and he held his sickle high!

Somehow I assumed that wrestling would be easier than what I was experiencing, and for some people maybe it is, but not for the ol' Edgemeister. When Swinger, and eventually Jay, joined the gym, they picked up the wrestling moves pretty quickly. I think I fell somewhere in between them. After joining the gym in May 1992, I never would have expected to be ready for my very first match on July 1, 1992.

Let's set the scene. It was hot, brutally hot (yes, it gets hot in Canada), and it was Canada Day. The match was taking place at Monarch Park nestled just off Sherborne Street, in Toronto, for a Canada Day celebration.

Of course, before the show started, we had to struggle through a scorching PTA session, in front of the audience, to show them a portion of our training. Finally, it was time. Time for my very first official match: a battle royal. Now, some people might say that a battle royal can't count as your first match. I say screw that. I got hit, took bumps, and damn it, I lasted to the final four, so in my eyes, it was a match. When it came to my ring attire I was sorely lacking, and it was actually pretty embarrassing. I was sporting some Oakland Raiders Zubaz and old-school Converse high-tops. I was mortified, but still I hopped into the ring (the very same ring I use to set up for the Orangeville indies). Man, am I glad I did, because getting in front of that audience was a life-altering experience.

I kept training. I promised myself that when I entered the ring from now on, I would look more professional than anyone else. I spent hours designing outfits. My girlfriend at the time bought me my very first pair of wrestling boots for my birthday. My look was very Bret Hart–influenced and I was ready to take the world by storm. My only problem was lack of funds. I was investing in wrestling but made no money in return. I had just graduated high school and it was time to get a full-time job and bring in some real money.

My place of employment was called Johnson Control, a factory in Orangeville that made car seats for Chryslers. I bought a 1987 Volkswagen Jetta, worked during the week, and wrestled on weekends. It was a tiring schedule, but I felt like things were on a roll. Until one fateful day.

During our shift, we had to build a certain number of seats or it was overtime, and strangely enough, none of us wanted to stick around. A yellow cage would come down to our work stations containing all the parts we needed, and then proceed upon its merry way to be filled once again on the other side of the factory.

One day the foreman decided to play a joke on one of the guys. He wanted to handcuff the unsuspecting victim to the cage, forcing him to circle the entire factory. Being the biggest guy on our line, the foreman came to me for help. He wanted me to pick the guy up, and hold him, while he and his accomplices handcuffed him. I agreed, and it worked. No one got hurt and it actually ended up being pretty funny. Unfortunately, the suits in the front office were not so pleased. Guess who the fall guy was? If you guessed the new guy—me—then you would be correct. I was devastated, and once again I was forced to stop paying my even more expensive car insurance. It was a huge risk to drive without insurance, but I had to get to wrestling class.

Looking back now, I can laugh. I didn't want to work in that factory for the rest of my life, it just wasn't for me. Who knows, if the incident didn't happen, I might have been stuck there building car seats until retirement and not have realized my dreams.

My first publicity shot, taken at Sully's Gym.

While I was busy concentrating on my fledgling wrestling career, my mom was struggling with our bills. Now I had no job and our financial situation was spiraling down the toilet faster than a Michelle Kwan triple lutz. While I looked for a job, we were forced to move from our apartment into the Panorama Motel, a bona fide dump. My mom waitressed at the restaurant connected to the motel, so at least we had one positive. I was eighteen years old and I felt like a useless piece of shit until I finally found two part-time jobs, one of them bouncing. I was able to keep up my wrestling training, work the occasional match, and help my mom again financially. We found an apartment and moved out of the motel. Things were starting to go smoothly again. I worked at a warehouse by day and bounced rednecks at night. Fatty reared his fat head and joined me bouncing at the bar. Technically, it was illegal, we were under age, but it was fun.

While this was going on I geared up for my second appearance at Monarch Park, once again on Canada Day. This time I was in a Handicap

Tag match. Shane Gallant, Rob, and myself versus American Gladiator (Keith) and "Dragon" Billy Johnson (Joe).

For some reason, the babyfaces had the numbers advantage, which I still don't understand, but oh well. I recently watched this match and it actually holds up all right. Up until that point of my career I was almost embarrassed when I entered the ring. On July 1, 1993, that began to change. The crowd reacted to me and actually chanted "Adam." Who cares if it was only a hundred people, I'd never heard that, and I was jacked. My method of looking like a pro was working. Now Joe, Keith, Swinger, Rob, and I took bookings where we could, when we could. We landed a booking for a promotion in Winnipeg called IWA Wrestling. They were doing TV tapings and needed some extra bodies. So Swinger, Joe, Keith, and I hopped on a bus for the thirty-hour trek to Winnipeg. This drive was brutal, but it highlighted what may have been my strangest encounter, and trust me, I've had some strange ones.

A Rastafarian with a strange gleam in his eye got on the bus in Sudbury, Ontario. He sat down, took out a piece of glass hidden under his red, green, yellow, and black knit hat, and began to talk to it. He was spinning it around, pouring a beer (which he not so secretly snuck on) all over it, and holding it up to his eyeball. It magnified his eyes, which looked really comical, but the dude was not right. I don't know what the hell he saw in that glass and I sure as hell did not want to find out. At about four A.M., still on the bus, Rasta took out a two-string guitar and commenced to serenade the bus. Problem was, he woke everyone up to do it. The bus driver told him to be quiet. He put the guitar away and I fell asleep to the sounds of Rasta saying he wouldn't let the man keep his music down.

I don't know what the hell he saw in that glass and I sure as hell did not want to find out.

Waking up to darkness I had an odd feeling, and with good reason. Rasta was face-to-face with the peacefully sleeping Swinger, and he was biting my style—he was growling like I had so many years before at my uncle. Somehow I had the distinct feeling he was not imitating Peter Criss; I think he was just utterly insane! I jumped, Swinger jumped, Crazy Marley screamed, and the bus driver not so politely told him to get off the bus—it was five A.M. with ten-foot snow banks in Wawa, Ontario—to more shouts of the man keeping him down. We survived the thirty-hour bus ride and arrived in Winnipeg for our three shows.

He taught me that a match did not have to be a prearranged spot fest . . . he taught me to have fun in the ring.

This was my first television exposure and it felt like the big time. The promoter was Tony Condello (a one of a kind, even in this business) and "The Natural" Don Callis was the booker. They had gotten a very professional look together for the old Walker Theater in downtown Winnipeg. I wrestled as Adam Impact, and I worked

With the IWA title, backstage at the Walker Theater in Winnipeg.

Joe and Swinger for the TV tapings. Both matches went well, so I was booked against one of the top heels for our last show. I wrestled Lenny Olsen (Dr. Luther), who ended up becoming a good friend and teacher in the ring. He taught me that a match did not have to be a prearranged spot fest, but more important, he taught me to have fun in the ring.

The trip was done. We had enough money to fly home, with about twenty dollars left over, so I definitely notched this trip up as a success.

CHAPTER

Just because I had money to fly home from Winnipeg did not mean I had an abundance of green (or purple, brown, red, and blue in Canada) occupying my wallet. As a matter of fact, we were still going meal to meal, so it was time to take a stab at another full-time job. Fatty's dad, Mike, had a hand in numerous companies, one of them being a shrink-wrap factory, so this became the place for me to ply my trade. The company was located in Oakville, about an hour from Orangeville, so once again I drove to work every day without insurance.

Once I got to work I drove a forklift. Being the only person on the floor who spoke English, the job became boring and tedious pretty quickly. Daydreams of wrestling at the SkyDome and Maple Leaf Gardens passed the time. It limited my wrestling bookings to weekends and close distances. Detroit, Windsor, Ajax, Whitby, Ottawa, and Toronto were about the extent of it.

While it did affect my wrestling career, the job did pay dividends at home. The bills were paid and food was on the table. However, I slowly felt myself falling into the factory-for-life rut I had always tried to avoid. Some people can do it and God bless them. As I've explained earlier, I am not one of those people. I feel I was put on this planet to entertain in one form or another, so with that in mind I applied to Humber College in Toronto for their radio broadcasting course. Now, wrestling was all I wanted, but working the indies, one never knew what might happen. I wanted a fallback option in the event I suffered a career-ending injury. Radio and music have entertained me endlessly throughout the years, so it seemed like a logical and fun choice.

While I awaited a reply from Humber, I still slugged away on my forklift. One morning on my way to work, during a particularly bad ice storm, I lost control of the Jetta on a back road. It spun out of control and left the road backward. It flew over a ditch and landed about fifteen feet into a farmer's field. Thankfully, all of the snow cushioned the impact and I was okay. What wasn't okay was the fact that I had fifteen feet of very deep snow between my car and the road. I dug myself out of the car and walked to the farmer's house. The lights were on, but apparently no one was home. Or they looked out the window, saw a six-foot-five, two-hundred-twenty-five-pound man, soaked to the bone, knocking on their door at six A.M. Take your pick.

A cellular phone was not in my financial realm, so I was left with only one option: dig myself out. After about two hours, and a slight case of pneumonia later, I was able to get the Jetta back to the ditch. The ditch would prove as insurmountable as Jonathan Coachman having an entertaining match. Finally, after about another hour, someone else was brave enough (or stupid enough) to drive down that barren back road. It was a pickup truck equipped with a chain, and I was pulled to safety. If you think I was a trooper and continued on to work, think again. I went home, had a cup of tea, some chicken noodle soup, and passed out to thoughts of Humber College acceptance slips arriving in the mail.

Finally, as I was nearing my one-year anniversary at the shrink-wrap factory and limited wrestling bookings, I received my college acceptance form. I would be the second person in my family to attend college! I decided to keep driving the forklift for extra tuition money until school started. I had applied and been approved for a student loan, but every penny would count.

I kept the job until my good buddy John Posavac called with an offer. How would I like to rent a house on—not in—Wasaga Beach, Ontario. That definitely got my attention, but here's the real kicker. I would work at a bikini shop for the summer! Regrettably, I had to politely decline the offer . . . okay, if you believed that, shame on you! I said **"Hell Yeah"** louder than a crowd at Stone Cold Steve Austin!

My last day of work had come and I had visions of bikinis bouncing in my head. Maybe that's why, after a sixteen-hour workday, a skid of Pepsi products that I had just stacked toppled over directly onto yours truly. I was safe in the confines of the forklift's cage, but I still took an orange soda shower. It was at this moment that I realized two things: one, at this point, sodas did not rule, and two, that I quit. I walked out of my forklift, punched out for the last time, and, while starting to resemble an orange popsicle, drove home.

CHAPTER

By now my mom and I had moved into an apartment right across the alley from our very first apartment. It was from this apartment, at the age of nineteen, that I moved out. It was time for me to make a go of it on my own. My mom was upset—I was moving out on Mother's Day—but she tried not to show it. Her little boy was growing up.

My main goal when I began wrestling was to buy my mom a house. As I backed out of the parking lot, waving good-bye to her, I vowed to make that goal become a reality. On the one-hour drive north to Wasaga Beach, I repeated my new mantra over and over, "Don't worry, Ma, I'm gonna

That's John in front of the infamous Wasaga beach house.

get you a house." I think it was my way of softening the blow of leaving home.

Now I was a single nineteen-year-old, working at a bikini shop, and renting a huge house on the beach with four other people, three of them complete strangers. They ended up being cool roommates, but I still spent most of my time with John. We rode our bikes to work every day and sold bikinis. It was about as tough as it sounds, and our libidos were running like Ferraris on the Autobahn. We definitely sowed some wild oats that summer, and sold a shitload of bikinis!

Our routine was to come home from work, eat, train, listen to Jimi Hendrix and Soundgarden, and attend toga parties. For some reason I still don't understand, toga parties seemed to be a nightly occasion in Wasaga Beach. I distinctly remember one such party. Our house was owned by Italians with bad taste, so our bedsheet selection was limited. I was sporting a sheet with huge turquoise-and-blue Hawaiian flowers all over it. Take my word for it, it was not a pretty sight. On this particular night we were joined by Jay and a few other guys, one of

We rode our bikes to work every day and sold bikinis. It was about as tough as it sounds . . .

them with the nifty little handle of Burt the Hurt. Why Burt the Hurt, you ask? It's pretty simple, Jay Brown (Burt's alter ego) has horrible eyesight. He read a wrestling flyer that said "Beat the Heat." To Burt's legally blind eyes it read Burt the Hurt, and a legend was born.

Burt the Hurt was an aspiring, but extremely clumsy, Sully's Gym trainee from Orangeville. He had developed a promo style that kept us in tears. He referred to himself in the third person long before The Rock, and on this night he had ample opportunity to use it.

We had left our house and piled into a vehicle known as the Flaming Wagon. A robin's-egg-blue station wagon with, appropriately enough, hand-painted flames all over it. It was about as horrendous as my bedsheet. When we got to the party, Burt got hammered, and the Hurt appeared as quickly as Bruce Banner becomes the Incredible Hulk. With the Incredible Hurt in full swing, we decided to leave the toga party. While the rest of the partygoers acted out biblical scenes on the front deck, we took this strange opportunity to go to Sunshine Park, a campground full of drunken women!

The only problem was a matter of money. It cost $45 a night to stay there. Once again, funds were lacking, so we decided to sneak in. To do this, we had to crawl through what felt like an impenetrable forest. We shimmied across the forest floor in our fluorescent bedsheets, trying to avoid detection by the bikers hired for guard duty. Finally, after what felt like hours, we were on the edge of the campgrounds. Over Burt muttering to himself in the third person, we heard the sound of girls partying, which sent our hormones racing, and rushed us into making a fatal error. We tried to make a break for it. Maybe it was the sound of five large men stampeding through the underbrush, or our bouncing neon flowers, but the bikers turned their flashlights on us. We had no choice, we had to turn back.

The bikers were hot on our heels, the illumination of their flashlights bouncing all over the dense forest, and I mean dense. Jay and I were hightailing it, ducking and dodging, until the forest, she overwhelmed us. Jay was ahead of me. He tripped and fell headfirst into a tree. Of course, I tripped over him and landed on him in a Kamala the Ugandan Headhunter–like splash. One of the bikers took this opportunity to strike. He swung for the fences with his trusty flashlight. I'm lucky I tripped over Jay, or the biker might have taken my head off. I rolled off the now moaning Jay, onto my back, and landed both feet to Easy Rider's sternum. He flew back, hit the closest tree, and decided that leaving was probably his best option. I corralled Jay and we took our time trudging through the rest of evergreen forest.

By the time we reached the Flaming Wagon everyone was back. Burt was in the backseat not looking too well. In fact, he was about the same color as the Hurricane's tights. We all jammed into the Flaming chariot, and readied ourselves for the short drive home. Before the car could get in motion, Burt the Hurt uttered the words that lifted him to legendary status within our motley crew. Burt, in his yellow-and-red toga, puked all over himself. His Technicolor launch, coupled with

"It looks like the hurt's all over Burt now."

the toga, was not a pretty sight. We were all fairly disgusted until Burt slurred, "It looks like the hurt's all over Burt now." How can you stay disgusted at something that ridiculous? We rolled down the windows and laughed all the way home.

The ref for this match—Adam Impact vs. Joe E. Legend—is Burt the Hurt.

Burt never made it in wrestling and, believe it or not, he's now a schoolteacher. That's a very scary thought, but just like Burt would say, "Just because the birds and the bees ain't singin', doesn't mean the sun ain't shinin' on the Hurt!" Long live Burt the Hurt!!

Another glorious sunset at Wasaga.

During that endless summer I had plenty of time to relax on the beach, and in my favorite discovery, a hammock-shaped tree branch large enough to hold me. Every day after work I would head down to my tree, Superunknown cassette blasting, and watch the sun set. This was my place to think, relax, and dream. It would also end up being the infamous location of a pretty good rib.

One early evening John, our visiting friends Alex Gawlik and Joe O'Gorman, and I were readying for, you guessed it, a toga party. Before we left John and Joe wanted to head to the beach. Once there, they decided to go skinny dipping. Now, unless a female is involved, I don't understand the appeal of skinny dipping. So, while John and Joe peeled off their togas next to my beloved tree, Alex and I hatched a scheme. John and Joe went running and screaming into the water while Alex and I took their togas and walked three blocks on a residential

Maple syrup, body hair, and mosquitoes in a Canadian summer are not a good combination.

street, back to the house. The sun was setting, so they were forced to run up the street in daylight, the way they were brought into this world, naked! Of course we locked the doors, so they were forced to do laps of the house to find a way in. We had turned the house into Fort Knox, so that was not gonna happen. Finally they gave up and knocked on the door. In the meantime, I devised the coup de grâce of our evil plan. When I opened the door, just a crack, I drew a bottle of maple syrup quicker than Billy the Kid with a .45. I doused the naked, sweaty bastards from head to toe. Maple syrup, body hair, and mosquitoes in a Canadian summer are not a good combination. After a few more sticky laps, and plenty of odd looks from the neighbors, we let them in. Thankfully, they never tried to get us back.

In between bikinis, pranks, and toga parties, I took wrestling bookings when and where I could. One such booking took place in Regent Park in Toronto. Little did I know that this show would have huge ramifications on my future. I assumed it was another small show, in front of another small crowd plus my mom and Fatty, and a chance to gain more experience. I ended up meeting a guy who would pop onto my radar screen frequently throughout the coming years. That guy's name was Sean Morley. On that show he was billed as the Canadian Combatant, although you may know him better as Val Venis. Sean seemed to be my closest competition to making World Wrestling Federation—and as you will read later, I was right. After the show Sean introduced me to some of his family, who had made the trek down from Peterborough, Ontario. I met his mom, his dad, and his sixteen-year-old Madonna-wannabe sister, Alanah. (Years later, that Madonna wannabe would end up being my wife!)

Close to the end of that wonderful summer, Fatty and Jay broke up with their girlfriends and became permanent fixtures at our beach house. I threw a couple of mattresses on the floor and put "Hotel California" on the stereo until we all crashed. Jay had a year of college, at Humber, under his belt, and finally decided to start his wrestling training at Sully's Gym. Actually, John, Jay, Fatty, and I all attended Humber that year. So, after our dream summer concluded, we decided, along with Johnny Newton, to rent a town house in Toronto.

That house became our unofficial frat house. A complete circus. We should have installed a revolving door for all the people we had coming and going. We tried, and I stress tried, to cook, and rarely did dishes. It looked like the house of five young bachelors. We were each assigned a week of dish duties. Invariably the dishes would get done on the first day, and after that be left to fester for a week until it was someone else's turn. We cleaned the house by having water-gun fights. You'd be surprised how well you can clean a filthy pigsty with a few water guns. During the year we all got on each other's nerves. It's to be expected, but no disagreements ever came to blows. However, this was when our five personalities started to move off in different directions.

You'd be surprised how well you can clean a filthy pigsty with a few water guns.

Johnny holed up in the basement like a maniac. John tried to bear down and got a serious girlfriend. Fatty eased along in his tattooed, eccentric way, and Jay more or less brushed off school to concentrate on wrestling. Meanwhile I landed a part-time job at Backstage Pass in the Square One mall in Mississauga. Backstage Pass sold vintage clothes and rock 'n' roll apparel, so once again I had landed a cool job. I also bounced and did my wrestling shows, so I ended up being busy.

Even with all of this, I was able to start and maintain a serious relationship with a girl named Diana I met in my radio broadcasting course.

College was proving to be fun. I was constantly exhausted, and still driving uninsured, but I was having a good time. Jay was taking to his wrestling training like the APA to beer, and everyone else was busy doing their own thing. But we would always meet in the living room for our Sega Genesis NHL Hockey tournaments. These were always hotly contested, and Jay, just like he is to *Raw* audiences today, was always the most annoying. He's always been able to get under people's skin—I think it's his special gift in life—but for these tournaments he had his annoying capabilities at full throttle. Many times these games would end with one, or all, of us storming off to our room. Hey, Sega hockey was important, dammit, and I never said we were mature!

That point became very evident quite a bit through the year. One night Fatty decided to go on a bender. He inhaled a bottle of Jamaican rum and became a belligerent bastard. Jay and I used this as an excuse for our next rib. When Fatty finally passed out on his bed, we crept in and pulled off his pants (not to worry, he still had his Underoos on). Fatty has black leg hair, so we decided to shave in the first word that came to mind: FAT. After admiring our new masterpiece, we left the room and quickly forgot about it. Until Fatty called us from his trip in L.A., which is where he discovered "FAT" shaved into his leg hair—while wearing shorts and walking down Rodeo Drive. Whoops!

This next one may not translate well to the written word, it was one of those you-had-to-be-there moments, but it's so stupid I have to mention it. There was a large crack under the bathroom door—it had to be a good two-inch gap. Of course, when any of us went in to drop the kids off at the pool, the rest of us would huddle on the stairs perfectly aligned with the crack and yell (in John's mother's very Croatian accent), "I can see your feet, you go poo-poo?" Suffice to say, it's tough to pinch a coil when you're laughing your head off, or maybe more appropriately ass, off. Now, while the women reading this may be disgusted, you have to realize that every guy goes through this phase. Thankfully, I've grown out of it (I think).

I was cruising along in college, but I never lost sight of my wrestling aspirations—it was still all I wanted. So when a three-week tour of Winnipeg became available I was going, school or not. Thankfully, my teachers were understanding and sympathetic to my plight. Diana would collect all of my homework and I'd work double time when I got home.

Swinger, Joe, and I made the trip. I assumed it would be like our last foray in Winnipeg. Man, was I wrong! I came completely unprepared for the icy hell on earth I would encounter. There were two positives

> **I came completely unprepared for the icy hell on earth I would encounter.**

to this trip: the invaluable experience I would gain, and the crew of guys who made the trip. We had Don Callus, Lenny Olsen (Dr. Luther), Jethro Hogg and his pet pig Snoots, Deathwolf Fenris (Paul Lazenby), a young Lance Storm, and the three of us (deemed the Toronto boys, even though Swinger is from Niagara Falls, New York).

We landed in Winterpeg (no, that's not a typo, trust me) and took a cab to our hotel. The Continental Hotel. Look up "dump" in the dictionary; they should have a picture of the Continental. It was on a par with the Panorama Motel. Little did I know that the Continental would hold the only bed I would sleep on throughout the whole tour. After a fitful sleep shared with cockroaches the size of Cadillacs, I found myself outside the hotel early the next morning waiting to be picked up to start the tour.

Finally, a white, extra-long Econo-Van pulled up with promoter Tony Condello behind the wheel. Even in the wrestling business Tony is one of a kind. As you'll see, Tony supplied plenty of laughs, usually at

We drove, drove, and drove some more.

his own expense. But before I get ahead of myself, we have to get back to our trip. We all piled into the van, new guys in the back. We, the Toronto Boys, were the new guys. I found myself scratching my head because the other guys were packing canned food and sleeping bags. I started to get a sinking feeling in the pit of my stomach, and it continued to sink as we drove, drove, and drove some more. Civilization was far behind us when we hit a bad invention known simply as "the winter road." I know it sounds like a bad eighties Cinderella power ballad, but it was much worse.

What's a "winter road," you ask? It's when a plow goes through a dense northern Canadian forest, leaving behind a rough, bumpy, pot-

I'd found hell on earth (outside of watching a Doink the Clown match).

hole-the-size-of-the-Grand-Canyon-filled path. All of this, plus the added feature of it being covered by ice and snow. *Yes!* Put it this way, the winter road portion was roughly one hundred sixty miles and it took twenty hours! I'd found hell on earth (outside of watching a Doink the Clown match). The weather was always thirty degrees Celsius or more . . . *below zero!* Add the windchill factor and you had frost forming on the inside of the van windows—but only in the back where the heaters did not reach. Remember who was sitting in the back? Yep, everybody's favorite Edgesicle! Of course, being the rocket scientist that I am, I also wore steel-toe combat boots. Not the best choice for keeping your feet warm. To make matters worse, every bump we hit sent our melons careening off the roof. If there was ever going to be a time that I was going to doubt my chosen career, it would have been on this trip. The great part was that I didn't doubt it once.

Obviously there were no restaurants on or anywhere near this cursed road, hence everyone bringing canned food. Everyone, that is, except for Swinger and me. Joe had a winter death tour under his belt, so he remembered to bring food, but he forgot to tell us. Joe is one of the most giving people I know, so he hooked us up.

After twenty-four hours we finally arrived at our first show at an Indian reservation called Oxford House. That name still sends shivers up my fused spine. With the windchill in full effect, the temperature was −72 Celsius, the coldest weather I have ever encountered. If you breathed through your nose, your nostrils would freeze together. If you breathed through your mouth, your lungs would not so calmly say, No way, asshole! The warning we had gotten was that thirty seconds of exposed skin would cause frostbite; so it was simple, you didn't go outside.

While on our pilgrimage north, a tragedy had befallen the small reservation. A teenager had gone out on the frozen lake with a gas can and huffed enough fumes to make his heart explode. As is the custom, the reservation shuts down completely for a week of mourning. You name it, and it shut down, including our show. We had three days till our next show with nowhere to go. So we stayed in the home ec room and gymnasium at the Oxford House school.

> **The temperature was −72 Celsius . . . Your lungs would not so calmly say, No way, asshole!**

Before the grocery store closed, Swinger and I went to get supplies. In order for truck drivers to be coerced into bringing food and supplies to these godforsaken places, they had to be paid extra. Probably the equivalent of P. Diddy's empire. It definitely went into the markup: for a can of tuna, $4; a bottle of Diet Pepsi, $6; and so on. Because of this I needed to take a draw (an advance on my salary), which gets you in a financial hole even before you've had your first show. To once again make matters worse (as if it was possible), one frigid night the power went out. The power lines had frozen. This meant no heat, in a school gym with no sleeping bag . . . did I mention it was—minus 72 outside! I got two words for ya, and they are not Degeneration X's "Suck it," they are *uh* and *oh*. We all took the blue gymnastics mats (our beds) and huddled together, hoping body heat would keep us warm. Finally the auxiliary power kicked in and we all breathed a sigh of relief, which, due to the temperature, we could actually see.

> **We all breathed a sigh of relief, which, due to the temperature, we could actually see.**

After our brutal Oxford House experience we moved on and finished the rest of the tour, but not before some classic ribs took place, all at the expense of our promoter, the Papa Geppetto–looking

Me and
Tony Condello.

Tony Condello. Tony is probably the most unintentionally funny person I've ever met. He can utter anything in his Italo-English hybrid language and have me in stitches.

On many of these death tours Tony would not bring a referee. The boys would pull double duty—wrestle and referee—until we finally put our foot down in a reservation dubbed Little Grand Rapids. What this meant was that Tony would now be our referee. He was also the announcer for our ring introductions, so not only would his brutal accent be on display, but so would his refereeing *in*abilities. Knowing all of this, Lenny, along with Don, hatched an evil but brilliant scheme.

They were able to nab Tony's very vibrant red sweatpants, which he wore to referee. While we distracted Tony, some Deep Heat ointment was lathered into the crotch of his pants. Now, Deep Heat gets pretty warm on your back and shoulders, so you can imagine what it would do to your nether regions, underwear or not.

"Ugh, I'm fuckin' dyin' in here! My balls is on fire!"

That night was a sellout. From the opening bell, we all gathered around the entranceway and watched Tony fidget and fondle himself. When it came time for my match, I approached Tony in the ring, and, in his one-of-a-kind accent, he said, "Ugh, I'm fuckin' dyin' in here! My balls is on fire!" After that, I could not keep a straight face.

It only got worse. Lenny was my opponent that night, and throughout the match we would "accidentally" bump Tony's flaming little tomatoes. Finally, the match was coming to an end. Tony could see the light of day. Or so he thought. I had mounted Lenny (in a manly way, of course) in the corner for the dreaded ten punches from hell. A staple in any legitimate babyface's repertoire to be sure, but this night it took an extra twist. When I finished doing my best Dave Grohl impression on Lenny's head, he commenced to do the classic Ric Flair face bump in front of Tony. The only problem, for Tony, was that Lenny had pulled his pants down on the way. Tony stood there in his little palm tree–covered bikini briefs in complete slack-jawed shock. By the time he realized what had happened, Lenny had a tight hold on the pants and would not let Tony pull them up. They fought harder than we did in the match. Tony's face was a deeper red than his pants. The crowd just giggled along with me, thinking it was part of the show.

That, however, was just the beginning. One of the guys on the tour, Jethro Hogg (who Tony mistakenly referred to as Jericho Hogg), brought a potbelly pig with him to the ring. His pig was named Snoots (Tony always mistakenly referred to it as Snooze), and Tony was scared to death of it. So that night Lenny and Don laid a trail of bread crumbs to Tony's bed (the ever-present blue gym mats), and also all over his cherished head of hair. Then they put yellow food coloring in his hair. All while he was sound asleep, and he didn't move an inch.

With baited breath, we all pretended to be sleeping and waited to see what would happen. Just like Mr. Burns releasing the hounds on Bart Simpson, they released the pig on Tony. It got on the bread-crumb trail immediately. It slowly grunted its way over to the snoring Condello, stopping to sniff his Deep Heat–laden crotch quite a bit, before moving on to the bread placed in his tight, now-yellow Afro. After about thirty seconds of the pig eating off his head, Tony was roused from his slumber and face-to-face with the dreaded Snoots. There was an uncomfortable silence and I swear I could hear a Clint Eastwood western soundtrack playing and tumbleweeds rolling by. It was high noon at three A.M. in Little Grand Rapids and the little Italian bastard lost it. He ran to the bathroom and screamed "the pig pissed on my head!" We lost it. Tears were streaming down our faces, we were laughing so hard. Tony came out of the bathroom, grabbed a hockey stick, and chased us around the gym, almost beheading Lance (who Tony mistakenly referred to as Land Storm, I kid you not), until he got winded, which didn't take long.

Usually, ribbing the promoter is not a good idea if you want to get paid.

Usually, ribbing the promoter is not a good idea if you want to get paid. Picture putting food coloring in Vince's coif, I don't think he'd be quite as understanding. Like I said, Tony is one of a kind, and luckily he had a good sense of humor at all the ribs directed at him.

We survived the rest of the trip, and actually made up the canceled Oxford House show at the end. This, once again, took twenty-four hours, bringing our total time driving to and from, and to and from Oxford House to ninety-six hours. All of this for the king's ransom of

I finished the tour with enough money for my flight home in admittedly rough shape . . . it was worth it.

$75. With the combination of the frigid weather, my steel-toe boots, and a lack of nourishment, I ended up getting strep throat. I finished the tour with enough money for my flight home in admittedly rough shape, but strange as it sounds, it was worth it.

CHAPTER

All of my roommates moved back home, so now I was truly on my own. I moved into a basement apartment about five minutes from school. While I was busy moving into my own digs that summer I also took all the wrestling bookings that were available. Once again I ran into Sean Morley, this time on the annual extravaganza (yes, that's my tongue firmly planted in cheek) known as the Tomato Fest. Why a festival based on celebrating tomatoes had a wrestling show is still beyond my grasp these many years later, but I took any chance I could to hop in the ol' squared circle. Sean and I got caught up on our travels and compared notes. He had been working full-time in Puerto Rico. I still looked at Sean as a star waiting to be found, and it looked like he was well on his way. I have to admit, it felt like he was passing me by. It motivated me to land as many tours as I could that summer. It also motivated me to make an embarrassing appearance on the *Dini Petty Show.*

For the uninformed, the *Dini Petty Show* was Canada's version of *Oprah.* I had only one reason to be there. One of my childhood idols, the best there is, the best there was, and the best there ever will be, Bret Hart, was a guest on the show. Joe and I managed to get tickets to the show and plopped ourselves down in the studio audience. As luck would have it, before the show, Dini informed the audience that Bret would take questions from the crowd. Hello! This was my shot to

> This was my shot to ask the one and only Hitman a question . . . to impress Bret.

ask the one and only Hitman a question. My opportunity to impress Bret. Show him I had some gumption. Hopefully enough to give me some advice on the wrestling industry. We told Dini we were aspiring wrestlers, so she told us we would get a chance to ask our questions.

Finally Bret came out, the championship title hanging over his shoulder. When it came time for us to ask our questions I was as nervous as a recovering alcoholic at an Oktoberfest. I most certainly came across as the wet-behind-the-ears greenhorn that I was. I managed to stammer out my earth-shattering question. I cut right to the chase. How do you make it? Bret had the same answer I now have for guys who ask me the same question. Get experience.

I was as nervous as a recovering alcoholic at an Oktoberfest.

After the show Joe and I came out of the washroom and came face-to-face with Bret. He actually stopped and took the time to apologize for not being able to help us more. That gesture has always stuck with me. Many of Bret's gestures would end up helping me in the future. With Bret's advice firmly lodged in my cranium, it was time to get more experience, and Winnipeg came calling again.

We lived on a steady diet of Kraft dinners and tuna fish.

Since these particular Winnipeg tours took place in the summer, there would be no dreaded twenty-four-hour winter-road drives. Instead of driving across lakes, we would be landing on them in pontoon planes. One four-seat plane went back and forth to the reservations transporting the boys and the ring. It took four separate trips from town to town to accomplish this, but we made it . . . barely. We had to balance the weight in the plane because it was so small. One crew consisted of the pilot, Joe, a midget, and me. Our little friend was named Chris, but he more closely resembled the Cryptkeeper. Even with the weight supposedly evened out we still felt every dip, shift, and wind current. I not so fondly remember grasping in vain at Joe and the Cryptkeeper as we dropped what the pilot later told us was two hundred feet.

The scenery in northern Manitoba and Ontario was breathtaking, but the reservations that we worked and stayed at were in rough shape. What else can you expect from a town named Bloodvein? We lived on a steady diet of Kraft dinners and tuna fish, and the beds we slept on were not exactly hygienic, so we were constantly checking for lice. You can imagine how that was with the mop on top of my head. Still, I was able to find some perks. During the day I would go fishing and cliff-diving. These places didn't have gyms, so workouts were nonexistent. Luckily Rob, Swinger, Keith, and Joe made the trips with me, so despite the constant fear of lice, no workouts, and hunger, the trips were fun.

This was the summer that marked my first trip to Detroit, Michigan. It was also the summer that Jay had his first match against Keith in the cozy confines of Sully's Gym in front of Fatty, myself, and maybe a dozen other people. He started making the Detroit shows along with the usual crew of misfits: Joe, Rob, and Keith. As a matter of fact, the Resos' Ford Taurus was affectionately dubbed Toby and routinely hauled us on the four-hour drive to Motown.

Joe and I finally stopped wrestling against each other and decided to form a tag team with the subtle name of Sex & Violence, Sexton Hardcastle and Joe E. Legend. The name Sexton Hardcastle finally reared its ugly head after I received Fatty's blessing. Jay and Keith formed a team known as Pride & Glory, Christian Cage and Zakk Wyld. With Pride & Glory as our opponents, Sex & Violence became a mainstay on the Michigan independent scene. We worked for Midwest Championship Wrestling and its "extreme" offspring, Insane Championship Wrestling. Around this time we met a guy who was just starting out, but had that special something you can't put your finger on. He wrestled as Terry Richards. D'Lo Brown (who was about to break out in his own right) rechristened him Rhino Richards, which he would later shorten to Rhyno.

It's a very little known fact that I actually wrestled for WCW at TV tapings at Universal Studios Orlando. I made the twenty-four-hour trip with Rhyno and it's where we cemented our friendship. Basically, I was down there to be a bump dummy, or the more politically correct term "enhancement talent." And I was skeptical. Rhyno had done it before and so had Swinger. They expressed some interest and the Swing Man actually got a contract out of it—the first of our gang to be signed. I met many people who, until they read this, won't even realize I worked a match there. I wrestled as Damien Stryker (my worst moniker to date) against Meng and Kevin Sullivan. During the match I got choke slammed on the rotating wooden platform the ring was on. This wasn't any ordinary choke slam. This was a choke slam from the Giant (now the Big Show). To this day no one remembers this except Rhyno and me, but it's in the WWE's vast video vault somewhere. This was my first and last trip done strictly for money and no career advancement. In those three days I got a bad vibe from WCW—that the inmates were running the asylum—and it further reinforced that World Wrestling Federation was the place for me.

The inmates were running the asylum . . .

Now it was time to enter my second and final year of college to complete my radio broadcasting course. I still kept my wrestling dreams alive by taking more winter death tours and a booking in Ajax, Ontario, which would have me wrestling, unbeknownst to me, in front of a man named Carl DeMarco. Carl would end up having a huge positive impact on my career and I consider him a friend to this day. I never forget who helped me on the way up.

> I never forget who helped me on the way up.

Ajax is basically a suburb east of Toronto and it was here that fate worked in my favor. A tiny crowd of about a hundred people (including a heckling Jay and Keith) saw Sex & Violence take on Swinger and Rob. Once again I crossed paths with Sean, who was not only booked in Puerto Rico, but now Mexico, too. (He was positive he saw me working down there. He was wrong, it was actually a guy named Chris Jericho who was already making waves. But let me get back to my story about fate intervening.) At this time Carl was Bret Hart's business manager, and he thought he saw something in Sean, Rob, and me. We kept in touch and shortly thereafter Carl took over the reins as World Wrestling Federation's Canadian president. Oh yeah, fate, she was smiling. Carl loved Rob's Jushin Liger–like outfit and Lucha Libre style. Because of this Rob got a call and was asked to head out to Sydney, Nova Scotia, to wrestle Hakushi, a Japanese wrestler who had "tattoo" stickers all over his torso. According to Rob, the match went okay, but Hakushi didn't speak English. (Rob still has yet to get his break. He has worked the occasional dark match for the company and he's opened a great wrestling school called Squared Circle Training in Toronto.)

As all of this was happening I was finishing up college. Diana and I were still together, and I was still working at Backstage Pass. On the wrestling horizon nothing monumental seemed about to happen. But like I would be so many times in the future, boy oh boy was I wrong!

Things were starting to look pretty bleak. I finished my schooling, quit my job at Backstage Pass, and moved to Rockwood, Ontario. A tiny hamlet ten minutes outside of Guelph, where I was scheduled to do my college internship. I had no job and was surviving on what little money I had left from my student loans. On top of all that, the Canadian government wanted their school loan repaid, which came to a total of $20,000. Let's just say I had the stress level of George Castanza from *Seinfeld*.

On the wrestling horizon nothing monumental seemed about to happen.

On May 10, 1996, I got a call from Jay that shot a ray of light through the dark clouds over my head. Apparently, Carl DeMarco was trying to contact me to work a match on a World Wrestling Federation show at Copps Coliseum in Hamilton. The same place where I sat enthralled so many times over the years. Now I had the problem of trying to get to Hamilton. That's when Jay and Tony the Taurus pulled my fat out of the fire. Jay picked up my mom, and then Diana and me, and we were off to Steeltown.

My opponent that night was Bob "Hardcore" Holly, although at that point he was still the Spark Plug, checker-flag tights and all. I arrived at the building three hours before the show, not realizing that for non-televised live events the guys show up about an hour before bell time. This gave me enough time to get good and nervous. Our match was scheduled first. The show started at 7:30 P.M. Bob, who showed up at 7 P.M., walked up to me and asked how long I had been working. I replied with the truth, three and a half years. I realized that honesty might have been the wrong approach when Bob rolled his eyes, grunted, and walked away. Knowing Bob the way I do now, I'd laugh. Back then, I said "shit," but vowed to prove that I belonged in the ring with him.

They asked me my ring name and timidly I said Sexton Hardcastle. That raised some eyebrows and guaranteed all the guys would be watching to see what I could do. I was nervous as hell. Who wouldn't be? I was the new kid, a twenty-two-year-old greenhorn. Jake "The Snake" Roberts, Razor Ramon, Vader, Ultimate Warrior, and all the rest were there to see if I would sink or swim. I was ready to show them I could swim nearby Lake Ontario.

What was my way of proving myself, you ask? One word: dancing. Extremely bad and extremely Caucasian. I mean white. Whiter than Kurt Angle eating a peanut butter and jelly sandwich on Wonder bread, followed by a piece of apple pie, all washed down with a big, frothy glass of homogenized milk. And that my friends is Clorox bleach white. You see, at this point, Sexton Hardcastle was teaming on the indies with Jay, who worked as Christian Cage, to form the Suicide Blondes. For some unknown reason we decided that dancing, very badly, would get a reaction from the crowd. So Jay would do the dance called "the Carlton" (from *Fresh Prince of Bel Air*) and moves very reminiscent of his future peeparoonie. In the meantime, I would display the most horrendous version of the running man you will ever see. With all of that being said, I thought that my debut was the perfect opportunity to use my Tide-white-like running man. I walked to the ring with the music I always used, "Walk" by Pantera, and the nerves disappeared. I climbed in the ring and looked down to the front row to see the look of pride on my mom's face. I smiled inside and started dancing like a madman. It looked like I was having a seizure.

The referee (and now good friend) Timmy White was dumbstruck. He later confided to me, in full Providence accent, that he was thinking, "What the hell is this kid doin'?" My mom snapped a picture of the spectacle her son was making of himself. She caught Timmy's incredulous look perfectly. To this day, I laugh when I see that picture.

> I smiled inside and started dancing like a madman. It looked like I was having a seizure.

Finally Bob hit the ring and it was time for him to stare at me in disbelief, and try not to laugh. Now, with Bob Holly, that's tough to do, and I think that won him over. Hey, if I was willing to make that much of a fool out of myself I must be okay. The match went great and the people were into it, even though they had no clue who Sexton Hardcastle was.

This was the beginning.

You can hear Timmy White thinking,
"Sexton Hardcastle??"

I came back through the curtain to congratulations from Jake, Warrior, and Razor. Jake said I had "it." Warrior said he loved it, and Razor was very helpful. He said now all I had to do was get used to working in front of ten thousand people as opposed to ten. Sounded good to me. The road agents Tony Garea and Rene Goulet were patting me on the back. George "The Animal" Steele said he'd see what he could do for me. My pay was $500 US, which meant I could survive a few more months.

Suddenly that thimble-sized light at the end of the tunnel was starting to grow in size. It was at least the size of my thumbnail, and getting bigger every day. All the skeptics who said that World Wrestling Federation and a wrestling career were a pipe dream shut up. As a matter of fact, most went from being skeptics to full-fledged supporters. Go figure.

was booked constantly in Detroit and on some more Tony Condello tours all over northern Ontario, Manitoba, and Saskatchewan. I was on the road, but not making much money. In Winnipeg I got $75 a show, in Detroit $100, and in Toronto I still set up and took down the ring and wrestled for free. With my meager earnings I couldn't keep living in Rockwood. This meant I had to pack up and move back home. Since I had moved out my mom had downgraded to a cheaper, but much smaller, bachelor apartment. We slapped the mattress on the floor and I was back at home in Orangeville. All the while my goal of buying my mom a house was constantly rattling around in my brain.

We were back to the days of not being able to afford a phone. Here I was, supposedly a man, but not being able to help out with the bills at all. If I took a day job I'd have to say no to bookings.

I was twenty-two without two pennies to rub together...

I was twenty-two without two pennies to rub together, but bless her heart, my mom never doubted me. She's definitely a special kind of lady to put up with me!

Shortly after the move back home Diana and I split up. She went to Montreal for her internship and I hit the highways to wrestle. Those highways led me to Cleveland, Ohio, where Swinger, Jay, Joe, and I got booked for two shows. Two shows that included a grand total of about fifty fans—I think there were more boys in the dressing room. Obviously, it wasn't a high-paying proposition, but once again, it was experience. It was also an opportunity to network, and Jay was able to find some shows for me and him in Tennessee. His heart was in the right place, but to this day I don't let him live down "the Tennessee Debacle."

Getting hardcore in the ICW; this is in Detroit.

After Cleveland we had a show in Niagara Falls, came home for time enough to repack, and stumbled upon the harsh realization that we had no money, but we still left for Tennessee. First we had a show in Detroit that would supply us with the monumental monetary funds— $75—to make it down south. After the show we hitched a ride to Kentucky with Cheech (Chi Chi Cruz) and met up with Jay's Tennessee contact—a guy named Allen. We were excited at the opportunity to go somewhere else. We definitely didn't take the time to think things through, and Jay took Allen at his word. I trusted Jay's usually good judgment. Besides, this was some experience in what felt like a foreign land, and hopefully we'd make enough money to get us back home just in time for Christmas. At least, that's what we thought.

After cramming into Allen's hatchback Dodge Charger, we slowly made our way to a little town known as Fall Branch. I had a sinking suspicion that a few things had fallen besides branches. Like IQs and cleanliness. Finally, after chain-listening to Lynyrd Skynyrd's *Greatest Hits*, we arrived. As cruel as it sounds, I wish we hadn't. I had an odd feeling about this trip from the get-go, and arriving at Allen's house confirmed those feelings. Now, I've lived under some less than stellar conditions, but at least we kept those conditions clean. The same could not be said about Allen's place. There was garbage covering the floors. Dishes were stacked to the ceiling. A backed-up sewagelike stench filled the house. A trail of ants were parading around the bathroom. It was the kind of place where you don't want to take your shoes off, let alone take a shower.

Dishes were stacked to the ceiling. A backed-up sewagelike stench filled the house.

This would have to go down as the worst month in the annals of my professional career. Just to add to an already lousy situation, it seemed Allen had heat with the entire state. His eighteen promised shows ended up being three, and one of those was in his father's barn up the road. We worked that one for free in front of six people sitting on bales of hay. The silence was deafening. Everyone has a low point in their career. That would have to be mine. The other two shows were spaced almost the entire month apart. By now we had around $50 each to survive the month. This meant our shows had to pay for our bus tickets home. Our slowly dwindling $50 left us with roughly $2.50 a day for food. Allen slept all day and hid whatever food he had. When Jay and I went to sleep, Allen would plop his obese frame in front of the TV, surround himself with junk food, and watch wrestling tapes all night. We used our rationed money to hike down to Fall Branch's only restaurant and purchase our meal for the day. A coffee and a burger. I get hungry just writing this story.

One night Jay and I hitched a ride to a wrestling show in nearby Johnson City. We got there and the Suicide Blondes were able to book themselves onto the show, for free of course. It wasn't a bad crowd and they ate up our long-haired, Canadian, white meat babyface schtick. Looking into the crowd that night I quickly realized one thing: The popularity of the mullet was firmly intact at a wrestling show in Johnson City, Tennessee. Now I was a full-on, former mulleteer. Eddie Guerrero had nothing on me. I proudly walked around with that feathered atrocity atop my skull for years. But you see, at some point I joined everyone else in the nineties and realized the error of my follicle flub.

The mullet hadn't made a comeback here, it had never left.

In the foothills of the Smoky Mountains people had not yet heard that the mullet had died a horrible death, thanks to grunge music. I don't mean to get off on a rant, but the mullet hadn't made a comeback here, it had never left. I mean, we were talking mullets, fullets (the female version), skullet (picture Paul Heyman), and quite possibly the worst form of physical and mental abuse you can heap upon a child . . . the bullet. Yes, believe it or not, folks, a baby mullet!

After this hairy experience we made our way back to Fall Branch to await our next show at the Armory. This show was memorable not for the payday of $10 but for the horrendous kendo stick shot I took to the berries. Not only had Allen promised us eighteen shows and lied, he was also the culprit who abused my boys with a kendo stick. Allen booked the show, and like most working bookers, put himself in the main event against two guys who could make his marginal talents look good. We were doing just that until he decided to carelessly swing at my unmentionables while I lay selling on the mat. This marked the most nausea I've ever felt in my life. It got replaced pretty quickly by anger and a Tennessee kendo curbstomp commenced. Few people have truly seen me lose my temper. I can keep it in check. You have to really piss me off. Mess with my family, my friends, or limit my chance at reproducing because of a kendo stick and you should duck and run. Allen realized this too late, and as he tried to roll under the bottom rope (which was impossible with his tremendous girth), Jay finally got me under control. Eventually, after I massaged myself back to comfort (hey, I didn't have a girlfriend), it ended up being water under the bridge. Because of our situation I had no other choice.

It was nearing Christmas and Jay and I both came down with a brutal flu. That whole not-eating thing probably fueled the flu's fire. We had two shows left and they were in North Carolina. This is when help came in the form of Tracey Smothers, who at the time was working for World Wrestling Federation as Freddy Joe Floyd. He was booked on these shows and picked Allen, Jay, and me up for the trip to Raleigh.

The first night in North Carolina we stayed at the house of the show's financial backer. We got there and I wished I was back in Fall Branch. The dude was a full-fledged KKK member. I'd never seen so much Dixie flag memorabilia. Jay and I were not used to much of this hateful bullshit up in Canada; so, realizing we didn't have any options, we quickly hit the sack as this Gomer downed whiskey out

The dude was a full-fledged KKK member.

of his rebel shot glass. Tracey also worked as the Wild Eyed Southern Boy, but he was just as uncomfortable as we were, and we took off for the show early the next day. After the show, Tracey left for his commitments, and we were able to land a hotel-room floor thanks to a wrestler named Major DeBeers. We worked our last match and, like Tennessee, North Carolina took to the Suicide Blondes. We still didn't make enough money to get home, so we made that tail-between-the-legs phone call home for help. Jay called home and his parents put enough for the bus ticket in his bank account. My mom had a phone now so I filled her in. She took the rent money for our bachelor apartment and put it in my account. We slept on another floor that night in some house we somehow ended up at. We hit the Greyhound bus terminal the next morning and bought our tickets for the long trip from Raleigh to Toronto.

Of course, to keep our bad luck rolling, we fell asleep and missed our bus. We finally boarded a bus that stopped in Richmond, Virginia, from Richmond to Washington. We had a layover and Jay had enough money left over to get a burger. I had no money at all, but I did have a can of tuna. One problem, no can opener. Somehow I was able to cut the top open with my keys and eat it by hand. That would be my single, solitary meal on what would end up being a thirty-six-hour trip. From Washington we rode to New York. It was six A.M. and we had two hours until our next bus, and we'd never been to NYC. We made our way to the streets and stared in wonder like the two small-town kids we were. Then a friendly New Yorker "asked" me for my money or ATM card. I told him "Trust me, buddy, I have no money and my bank account won't help ya." Realizing Jay and I were not in the best of moods, he thought better of his idea and took off.

We made our bus from NYC to Syracuse, to Buffalo, to London, Ontario, and finally to Toronto and the waiting bear hug of Mr. Reso. I've never been so happy to see that jolly, bald-headed bastard! I arrived home Christmas Eve, about fifteen pounds lighter, to a home-cooked meal of my mom's stick-to-the-ribs stew and dumplings. Looking back at my Tennessee adventure I can laugh. Not a hearty guffaw, more like a reserved chuckle. *Ah screw it,* it sucked no matter what I say!

While some of my family and friends laughed and doubted my career choice, I soldiered on. Failure was not an option and it was too late for me to turn back. When I got home from Tennessee my mom fattened me up for what would be my toughest winter death tour yet. Yep, even worse than the first. This one was in January and the crew consisted of Jay, Rob, Joe, Keith, Cheech, and, breaking his death tour cherry, Rhyno. He had no clue what we had gotten him into.

> Failure was not an option and it was too late for me to turn back.

This once again meant another tour of reservations via the dreaded winter roads. On the way up, while bouncing over hurdle-sized bumps, one of our two vans broke down. Breaking down out there can mean death, but luckily the other van passed by shortly after. Jay and I were voted to go ahead with that van, while everyone else stacked themselves into the ring van. Jay and I hopped in the back of the passing van and sat among several open gas canisters. We arrived at the reservation six hours later, having inhaled enough fumes to give Cheech & Chong a buzz.

By the next night our passenger van was still not fixed, so Jay and I piled in with the others in the ring van. Picture a wrestling ring, all of our bags, and eight wrestlers literally stacked on top of one another in a utility van. I remember being crammed beside Keith with no room to move, my nose an inch from the roof, lying straight out. We could not move and if we had an accident we would have been done for. Luckily we made it through virtually unscathed, until our final show at a reservation called God's Lake Narrow.

After the show we decided we wanted to leave the frozen tundra of northern Manitoba behind and make the twenty-hour drive south to

87

the balmy subzero climates of Winnipeg. Tony wanted to stay the night, but we were sick of making Kraft dinners in the home economics room and sleeping on blue gym mats. Visions of dumpy beds and $2.99 all-you-can-eat pasta danced in our heads. Because of this I offered to take the first driving shift and we'd alternate nonstop until we reached Winnipeg.

It was the biggest lake I had ever driven across . . . It was pretty damn creepy.

To get off God's Lake Narrow we had to drive across a lake. This lake took an hour to cross at sixty km (37 mph) an hour. It was the biggest lake I had ever driven across (that sentence just sounds all sorts of wrong). It was a full moon at midnight on a frozen lake with no land as far as the eye could see. It was pretty damn creepy. I had to follow orange pylons to stay on the supposedly safe parts of the lake, all the while it made cracking noises. The locals said it was just currents under the ice, which of course didn't make me feel any better at all. However, due to my superior driving skills we made it over the lake in a little over an hour.

Later, at about four A.M., I was drowsy, even with Pantera blaring from the speakers to keep me awake. Just about this time I noticed that we were approaching our last lake to cross. There was only one problem: a football field–size hole filled with water between us and the shore! I shook my head to clear the cobwebs and hoped I was seeing things. I wasn't. I pumped the brakes while screaming every expletive known to man. Before I got the van stopped, my full load of suddenly awake wrestlers were piling out onto the ice. The ring van behind us—still carrying the ring, our clothes, and three wrestlers—was able to stop before hitting us. Now, besides a troupe of wrestlers, no one is stupid enough to be on these "roads," quite possibly for the entire winter, so we found ourselves in some major trouble (as in "possible death").

We all stood on the partially frozen lake at four A.M. in minus-fifty-degree-Celsius weather looking on in slack-jawed shock at this gaping hole. Finally, Tony, in his infinite wisdom, decided it would be safe to drive across. He found a stick, jammed it in the icy water, and it was only about a foot deep. Only my ass! It could drop off at any point! That was enough for me, so I tossed the keys to Tony and said, "Go crazy, boss," although I thought he was already there. Rhyno, Jay, Rob, and I all jammed back in the van while Tony acted like he had the situation firmly under control. Suddenly, *wham!* He gunned it, and we were off, at about two miles per hour. We dropped into the hole and set off about as fast as a flock of turtles. The water was freezing and hitting the bottom of the van. We were redlining and about to stall. All of us were screaming in Tony's ears, while Pantera still screamed from the speakers, but I'll hand it to the little Italian bastard, he got us across the hundred yards or so. I think Rhyno actually got out and kissed the snow-covered ground.

This brought us to our next dilemma: the much heavier ring van. It was being driven by a wrestler named Brian Jewel, and his plan was different from Tony's. There was actually a small, clear path to the shore beside the hole, and he decided that was the way to go. By this point we had all walked along the path back to the ring van in case they needed any help. Tony tried to tell Brian it was the wrong way to go, to no avail. He got about two feet and dropped through the ice up to the wheel wells, while still driving forward, deeper and deeper. Water was shooting everywhere, and it was damn cold. We're talking hypothermia cold. So Keith, Joe, and Cheech all scrambled out of the ring van, trying to dodge the water. Just then, something even more surreal happened.

Water was shooting everywhere, and it was damn cold.

I was standing next to Jay, when suddenly he just dropped, like someone had cut his legs off. At first I thought he slipped on the ice. Nope, he fell through the ice up to his thighs and that's when all hell really broke loose! Now I can look back at this and laugh my ass off, but at the time it was pretty scary (although the heel in me was still laughing). Seeing this finally sent Rhyno over the edge (bad pun intended). He saw Jay go through and hightailed it. He looked like Roadrunner, his thick, stumpy legs were spinning so fast. The only problem was, in his Tasmanian Devil–like panic, he took off in the wrong direction, back to God's Lake Narrow. By the time he got his mental compass back and realized his mistake, Jay was pulling himself out of the murky depths. As we got Jay to his feet, Rhyno stampeded by us and knocked him on his soaked ass again. I think that was the birth of the Gore. It was a comedy of errors. Rhyno weighed three hundred twenty-five pounds at the time. I've never seen a man so thick move so fast. As Jay spun around like a frozen top, Rhyno blazed back to the safe van.

Jay walked back to the van while his pants and boots quickly froze to his legs. The rest of us got footholds on what ice was left and, while still dodging geysers of water, tried to push the ring van back the ten feet to solid ice. Finally, between Joe, Rob, Keith, Cheech, and I, we were able to get it back to the point where it first broke through. Now we had to try and push it up about two feet onto solid ice again. By now, it was 4:30 A.M. We were tired and frozen and we just couldn't do it. This is where the tag line "Get the Rhyno" came from. He was the strongest dude on the tour, so I went to fetch the mangy Man-Beast.

When I got back to the safe van I found Jay with his bare feet on the heating vents, teeth chattering away, while his boots and socks sat on the floor, frozen straight up. Rhyno was in the middle row of seats, swaying back and forth and muttering like Dustin Hoffman in *Rain Man.* His muttering was actually praying. He honestly thought we were going to die on this frozen lake in the middle of a forest in northern Manitoba. He was the only American on the trip, so he wasn't quite used to this. Finally, I got him to let go of his death grip on the seat and walked him back to the lake, arm in arm like a little old lady crossing the street. Once I got him down there the Man-Beast kicked in and helped us push that bad boy out. By now the sun was starting to peek over the trees. The ring van took Tony's route and made it through. We were back on our way by 5:30 A.M., dethawing all the way to Winnipeg.

I'd like to say that this was my last winter death tour, but it wasn't. All in all, I did about twenty of these trips, but it was all worth it. It's where I cut my teeth in this business and I made some great friends along the way. Tony, Don Callis, Bad News Brown, Gerry Morrow, Johnny Smith, Cheech, Lenny, and my first meeting with two fellas by the names of Chris Jericho and Lance Storm. Most of these guys were smart and only did Tony's TV tapings. What can I say? I'm a glutton for punishment.

One day, while lounging at home on my floor-dwelling mattress between tours, I got a call from Carl DeMarco. Carl had an idea. The World Wrestling Federation Champion Bret "Hitman" Hart had gone down with a knee injury and subsequent surgery. Carl thought it would be a good idea for me to head out to Calgary and show Bret what I could do in the ring. It sounded like a great idea except for the obstacles in my way. My voyage wouldn't be smooth. I had no car and not enough funds to fly there, so my mom and grandparents pitched in the rest. So, thanks to my family, I was on my way to the home of *Stampede Wrestling*. The next problem was I had no place to stay. Bret had said it was cool to train at his house, but I didn't know him, so I didn't feel comfortable asking if I could stay there. Chris Jericho had an apartment in Calgary, but I knew he was in Mexico, and I didn't have his number. Lance Storm and I didn't know each other well enough at this point, and he was busy starting a family. I had one last hope: Johnny Smith.

Atlantic Grand Prix Wrestling with Bad News Brown.

I had met Johnny only twice before, but grew up watching him start his career in *Stampede*. We had worked together for Tony, and later we both ended up booked on a small show in Boston. On that show Johnny wrestled Jay and I wrestled a young Scott Taylor, the future Scotty 2 Hotty. Just to give you an idea of how "professional" this show was, our ring bell doubled as an ashtray. A ballroom is not the ideal place to run a wrestling show, but I had a great time working with Scotty and getting to know Johnny.

Yes, it is going to be painful.

I still didn't feel I knew Johnny well enough to ask to stay at his place, but panic mode was starting to kick in. My choices were non-existent, so I called him. I was very uncomfortable doing it, but he put me at ease right away. Although he barely knew me, he offered to take me in. That's just the way the wrestling fraternity is. Sure, there's all kinds of political bullshit, but when the chips are down we watch one another's backs. Johnny picked me up at the airport, gave me a bed, all the food I could eat, and drove me to Bret's every day. He refused to take my measly offers to pay. I owe Johnny a debt of gratitude, because without him, it would have taken me longer to get where I am today.

Now I had two full weeks in Calgary before a full summer of bookings in the Canadian Maritimes. Bookings were becoming easier to get as word got around about this kid from Toronto that World Wrestling Federation was interested in. But before that I had two weeks to try and impress Bret. He had a ring set up at the end of his indoor swimming pool room. There were already a few guys training there, under the tutelage of Bret and Leo "The Lion" Burke. Ken Shamrock and Mark Henry were brand new to the business and being put through their paces. I can't remember everyone who was there, but I quickly noticed one guy (in a manly way of course) in particular. He was tall, had a good build, and long blond hair. That guy was Andrew Martin, who has become better known as Test. At this point he'd never had a match, but after sizing each other up we clicked real good in the ring. Good enough that Bret told me to come back out after my summer tour for Atlantic Grand Prix Wrestling.

After thanking Bret, Leo, and Johnny, I flew home to pack up and hop in a Jeep Cherokee with my buddy Scott D'Amore for a drive to Shediac, New Brunswick. A mere eighteen-hour drive away. We drove straight through and began what would be a summer full of fun, but more importantly, experience.

At the beginning of my career I had almost reverted back to the shyness of my public school days. I'd look at my feet instead of the crowd. I was the black hole of charisma. Yet by the time I hit Shediac, I was a different wrestler. I'd been gaining experience and confidence, and the name Sexton Hardcastle was beginning to make minor waves. Wrestling seven to eight times a week was only going to help my cause. When Scott and I checked into our new home, the Shediac Hotel, I found out I'd be working in the main events against Bad News Allen (Brown). It seemed Mike Shaw (Bastion Booger) had pulled a no-show and News needed an opponent. I had done a few tours with News but didn't know him too well. Ya see, Bad News had a reputation for coming by his name honestly. He has an Olympic bronze medal in judo and is one pretty intimidating brother.

> I was the black hole of charisma.

93

Luckily we clicked in the ring, and he taught me . . . seven nights a week. Half the time the crowd would cheer him. He'd been on TV fighting the likes of Bret, Hulk, Piper, and the Macho Man. I would have cheered him, too. So we'd switch roles mid-match depending on the crowd. It helped to work on the fly and adjust. We hit every town in Nova Scotia, Prince Edward Island, Quebec, and New Brunswick. If you look at a map of Atlantic Canada and pick any town, I've been there. As serious as News looks in the ring, I always found some way to have him and our referee Frank "The Tank" Parker laughing. Once News starts laughing in the ring, he can't stop. He tries to cover his face like Curly from the Three Stooges, but to no avail. We had fun. The audience could range from twenty people to two hundred. I became a sponge. I gained invaluable experience working with News, and also watching veteran Rip Rogers work. Rip could get such heat by doing so little, and in our business that's a compliment.

If you look at a map of Atlantic Canada and pick any town, I've been there.

Two weeks into the tour Jay was added to the circuit. Scott and I moved out of the Shediac Hotel and found an apartment on the grounds of the University of Moncton to share with Jay. Most of the students had gone home for the summer and the building was virtually empty. Three other guys from our crew lived in the apartment across the parking lot—Rodney Blackbeard (believe it or not, his legit name), former CFL football star Glenn Kulka, and the late Mike Lozanski. The six of us would pile into Scott's Cherokee and drive three hundred miles to a show. We had to drive back to Moncton afterward because we couldn't afford hotel rooms and rent. On the rare occasion we did get a hotel room, there would be eight of us strewn about the room. It was basically a rugby scrum to get the best locations.

We were having fun logging miles, and little by little, I was starting to make some money. For the last month of the tour Rick Martel came in with Don Callis to form the tag team the Supermodels. They were trying to get ready for a run in World Wrestling Federation (which never materialized). This meant that the Suicide Blondes were reborn to take on the Supermodels and go around the horn in the main event. Night in, night out, we put in at least thirty minutes. Some nights we went close to an hour. That was Rick Martel's work ethic. He wanted to get in ring shape for his final run.

Landing on your head for a living tends to affect the ol' memory banks, and I know I've forgotten many stories from my East Coast excursion. I do remember being shoved in a Ford Escort station wagon along with five other wrestlers and one very pregnant woman. Rip Rogers took this trip with us and brought his extremely swollen wife with him. Rip

Landing on your head for a living tends to affect the ol' memory banks . . .

had quite a few road rules, including: live on two dollars a day and make no stops once you start driving except for gas. In other words, release your bowels before you get in the car. This didn't mean Rip had an iron bladder. Oh no, instead, he would roll out his member and piss in his protein shaker. All while his bulbous wife sat on his lap. I was sitting behind him, and let's just say I found it disturbing. Poor Scott was driving and witnessed this bizarre spectacle. It was like a car wreck. You don't want to look, but you do. I think it scarred him for life. It gets worse. When we got to the arena Rip rinsed the shaker and mixed a new shake. *Blah!!!* What can I say? I love Rip, but he is

It was like a car wreck. You don't want to look, but you do.

one demented dude, and if he offers his protein shaker, say no!

The final night of the tour took place in New Glasgow, Nova Scotia. The end of a tour is a chance to let your hair down and have some fun. It quickly became a night for memorable ribs. The last match of the night was scheduled to be the Suicide Blondes vs. the Supermodels. However, that night it was Rick Martel and a shrunken, Caucasian, long-brown-haired version of Abdullah the Butcher. Don had taken his black workout pants, put a string of masking tape with "A. Butcher" written on it, and stuck it on his hip. Or at least where his hip should have been, because like Abdullah, Don had pulled his pants up to just south of his nipples. He had actually taken the time to make black tape, curly toe extensions for his boots. It still stands out as one of the most ridiculous things I have ever seen in a wrestling ring, even more ridiculous than the Coach. Don's wrestling repertoire that night consisted of one move— Abdullah's judo thrust to the throat. That was it.

Luckily, Jay and I had a little rib of our own up our sleeves. We got our hands on the *Wrestling Album Vol. 2* supplied by our referee that night, Frank "The Tank." This cassette contained the horribly classic song "Girls in Cars." The theme music of former Tag Team Champions, Strike Force—Rick and his former partner Tito Santana. While "Girls in Cars" blared from the lousy New Glasgow sound system, Jay and I put on our best Rick Martel impression. We had our laces hanging out, and our "Martel babyface shuffle" was in full effect. We did all of Rick's signature moves including a double Boston crab. Essentially it was Abdullah the Butcher and Rick Martel vs. Rick Martel and Rick Martel. Don stunned us, we stunned Rick, and the crowd sat in stunned silence. The real winner that night was our referee Frank, who laughed through tears the entire match. I hate to admit it, but the best rib of the night was Don's.

Up until that point of my career I had never "bladed." The time-honored tradition of cutting yourself to get that infamous crimson mask. I always told myself I wouldn't do it until it meant something and added drama and heat to an angle. This meant it would not happen on the indies and definitely not in New Glasgow, Nova Scotia. I guess I'm not "hardcore," but I considered it pointless. Well, this night Don pounced on me like a large, uncoordinated cat while I was selling and started scratching away at my forehead à la the Butcher. I thought, "This bastard just gigged [cut] me," and I felt my forehead to check for blood. I came away clean and looked at Don's fingertips to see that he had taped pieces of coffee cup lids to his fingers. All while he cackled like an ugly hyena. He destroyed our rib, dammit, and while it wasn't a mat classic, it *barely* resembled a match, we had fun.

The tour was done, so Scott, Jay, and I jumped in the Cherokee and drove home. In the meantime I had talked to Bret about bringing Jay with me to Calgary. He said he was fine with that. We got back to Orangeville, where my mom had moved from the bachelor pad to a tiny town house, and packed. We used our Grand Prix savings to fly to Calgary for two weeks until our next Condello Manitoba/Ontario tour.

At least this time I arranged a place to stay. Michelle Billington, Bret's sister-in-law and the Dynamite Kid's ex-wife, said we could stay

The Suicide Blondes.

in her basement. Andrew was still training at Bret's and living there, but now he had to deal with Jay and me as roommates. Surprisingly, the three of us didn't kill one another, and we actually started a great friendship with Andrew that has lasted to this day. In those few weeks I fulfilled one of my dreams when I locked up and exchanged holds with one of my Big Three, Bret Hart (Shawn Michaels and Hulk Hogan being the other two). We would never get a chance to work with each other, but this was still damn cool, and maybe the next best thing. I had gone from sitting in the audience at the *Dini Petty Show* waiting to ask Bret a question, to exchanging holds with him in his ring, at his home.

This was a man I'd watched take part in some of the best matches I'd ever seen, and he was telling me I was ready!

By the end of the two weeks Bret told me, "I'm gonna talk to J.R. I think you're ready." This was a man I'd watched take part in some of the best matches I'd ever seen, and he was telling me I was ready! Not only that, but I had the World Champ going to bat for me to get a contract! I shook his hand and thanked him profusely. Jay and I headed to Winnipeg for our upcoming tour.

It was a summer northern tour. Those pontoon planes again. By this point I was flying so high on the adrenaline of Bret's words that nothing could bring me down, not even the death traps I was flying in. My mind-set of failure not being an option was finally paying off. I spent most of my time on this trip fishing and thinking about the future. After one of my fishing expeditions I called home and learned that Carl DeMarco had called, and it was important that I call him back ASAP.

Because I didn't have a cell phone, I found myself standing in the sheriff's office of Cat's Lake, Ontario (it was one of two phones on the reservation). I called Carl at World Wrestling Federation's Canadian offices. Carl told me J.R. had a contract with my name on it waiting to be signed in Stamford, Connecticut. The news didn't sink in. I know it's a cliché, but I couldn't believe my ears. It was mind-boggling. I was boggled, totally and completely boggled. (I had to buy

I know it's a cliché, but I couldn't believe my ears.

a vowel, because, **O** my God, this was amazing news!) The news I'd waited and wanted to hear since I was eight years old. I thanked Carl for the best news of my life, hung up, and hugged that chubby little

Italian wrestling promoter Tony Condello until he was blue in the face. Tony was just as excited for me.

I wanted to scream like Leonardo DiCaprio in *Titanic,* "I'm the king of the world," but I also didn't want to come across as a braggart. The rest of the guys were slugging away just as hard as I was, but they didn't have a contract signing to look forward to. I simply told everyone the news and tried to suppress my smile. Until I saw them smile. Suddenly being hugged by large men didn't bother me.

Some people don't believe in fate; I do. As kind as fate has been to me, it's also thrown some hurdles in there, too. In the middle of this summer tour, I caught the flu. I had a tour to finish though and hopefully it would help me sweat it out. That didn't happen. It got worse, but my flight to Stamford, Connecticut, was booked and I was not going to let the damn flu keep me from this opportunity. Anything less than a bullet between the eyes wouldn't have done it. I landed in New York's LaGuardia Airport and the company had a town car waiting for me. I'd never even seen the inside of a town car let alone rode to a beautiful hotel in one! I crashed like a ton of bricks hoping I'd feel better by morning.

> I was not going to let the damn flu keep me from this opportunity. Anything less than a bullet between the eyes wouldn't have done it.

I didn't feel better by morning. In fact, I felt worse as I prepared myself to go to the company's television studios, where a ring was set up. I arrived and, for a week, stumbled my way through matches with Tom Prichard and Michael Hayes. The matches were taped, and while I had taped all my indy matches, I knew this tape would be judged by different, harsher critics. Michael later confided to me that after I didn't complain about quite possibly the stiffest left jab, DDT combination in the annals of wrestling history, he told the office this kid was good.

At the end of the week, I was called to J.R.'s office, and even after my brutal weeklong performance, he had a developmental contract waiting for me. J.R. told me the sky was the limit, it was up to me. He told me to take the contract, get a lawyer to look at it, and send it back. I took it to my hotel, signed it, and brought it back the next day. Most people would call me a dumb ass (most still do), but I was twenty-three and this was my dream.

My developmental deal was worth $210 US a week or $300 Canadian. Not the numbers that were in my dream, but I had to start somewhere. Besides I could finally help out my ma on a regular basis. J.R. also told me to take as many indy dates as I could to keep the ring rust off until they had an idea for me.

Sex (me) & Violence (that's Joe E. Legend) with "Handsome" Johnny Bradford.

By now Joe, Jay, Rhyno, Bill Skullion, and I had a unit in ICW out of Detroit, called Thug Life. This was when the future Doctor of Thuganomics, John Cena, was probably just hitting puberty. We had wrestling's only deaf manager, the illustrious, "Handsome" Johnny Bradford. We made Rhyno an honorary Canadian and made Thug Life an anti-American group just before The Hart Foundation did it on TV.

Joe and I, as Sex & Violence, had some brutal matches with Mosh & Thrasher, the Headbangers. A stipulation finally banned all other Thug Life members from ringside. We decided it would be funny to dress Rhyno in black hot shorts and call him Chyno to run interference. The ICW brain trust thought a six-foot, three-hundred-twenty-five-pound man in hot shorts might be a bad idea, and nipped it in the bud. Eventually I started teaming with Jay in Detroit, which started a storyline tug-of-war between Joe and Jay, all for little ol' me as a partner. Jay and I turned on Joe, and the Suicide Blondes rode again, this time as heels. We had fun on these shows (a recurring theme, I know) and afterward always ended up at Rhyno's place to crash.

This next story is strange but true. When we went to Rhyno's house, finding a place to sleep could be a battle. He had a couch, but it was always occupied by his brother's friend, who had a snore that shook the foundations of the house. Rhyno also had a cot, or you could share his bed with him. Well, one night Jay nabbed the cot before I could. I used the old standard "I've been in the business longer than you" routine to no avail. This left me with two options. Sleep on the floor, or share the bed with the Man-Beast. I bit the bullet and decided to bunk with Rhyno.

When I went to sleep there was a good distance between us and I quickly crashed. When I woke later I found that Rhyno had closed the gap, and I was being spooned by the snoring, big, burly bastard! He was nuzzled up against me like I was his Mama rhino and he wanted to suckle my teat. What the hell! It was one of those moments. I dipped into my most manly voice, and yelled, "Get the fuck off me, ya horny freak!" Rhyno still brags to his wife (yes, he married a woman) that I am the first person, of either gender, he has ever spooned with. It doesn't exactly stand out on my résumé, but what the hell, it's still a first.

"Get the fuck off me, ya horny freak!"

101

"The Canadian what?"

Things were rolling along nicely in my career. I had a small, but steady income, taking what bookings were available with the company's blessings. One day I got a call from Bad News and Gerry Morrow asking if Jay and I would like to head over to Japan. New Tokyo Pro Wrestling needed a tag team and News and Gerry thought of us. We said yes and flew from Toronto to Calgary, where we met News and Gerry, and on to Vancouver, our final stop before an eighteen-hour journey to Tokyo. I was too excited to be tired and found myself walking around the tiny alleys, horrible traffic, and extremely short people right after I checked in. I felt like Godzilla wearing a blond wig as I looked down at cute little grandmothers who came up to my elbow. Cute yes, but they probably could have gone ninja and kicked my ass at the drop of a chopstick!

I felt like Godzilla wearing a blond wig . . .

Our first show was at the legendary Korakuen Hall. All Japan Wrestling ran a sold-out show there an hour before us, and we talked to some of their guys, like Johnny Ace and my old savior Johnny Smith. Jay and I had sent tapes and almost got booked there. I guess our tape is watched on the All Japan bus to this day. I hope everyone gets a good laugh because, looking back now, it pretty much sucked. Our show that night was sold out as well, and Jay and I were eager to get out there and impress. We were booked against Leatherface and a Japanese wrestler whose name escapes me. We walked out in awe. We were even more awestruck when we were announced as "Adam & Gei, Canadian Hockey!!" Huh? Come again. Canadian Hockey? I have a funny picture of our reaction to our ring introduction. We later found out that, because of the accent, we misunderstood our name. We were actually the Canadian Rockies. Still pretty brutal, but I wasn't complaining.

It was a different style, but we adapted, did our thing, and the crowd and office were pleased. Pleased enough to promise us another tour. We flew back a month later for a tag team tournament to crown the first ever New Tokyo Pro Tag Team Champions. We won the tournament, but we were also the last New Tokyo Pro Tag Team Champions. The company folded soon after, but we left with a new style and more experience under our belts (not the tag titles, they kept those). I've since been back to Japan for WWE and always look forward to going. The Japanese really respect what we do, and are rabid wrestling fans. After my experience in the Land of the Rising Sun, it was time to head back to my mom's tiny town house and wait for that fateful and hopeful call up to the big leagues.

> **The Japanese really respect what we do, and are rabid wrestling fans.**

That fall I was booked on a tour of northern Ontario with Jay, Glenn Kulka, Cheech, and some others for a guy named Ike Shaw. We got on a remodeled school bus with bunk beds built into it. A poor rock star's rolling caravan. We started our trek north with an eight-hour bus ride, followed by a four-hour train ride. From there we hopped on a four-seater "boat taxi"—all while it was snowing. We crossed four at a time while everyone else froze on the lakeshore. I was just happy that for once we weren't driving across it. This process took another two hours. All to get to the thriving metropolis of Moose Factory, Ontario. Yes, you read that correctly— by now you should be used to names like this.

The only significant happening on this tour was that I escaped Moose Factory with my very first dog. Joe had seen two little girls trying to help a small puppy. Its parents had frozen to death, it was alone, and had no home. Joe brought that little husky back to our living quarters and she quickly became a fixture. As a matter of fact, she slept on my chest that and every night after. Basically, she picked me as her owner and I named her Frisco. Now I just had to get her back home. I had to sneak her onto the train in the armpit of my jacket. After that, she slept on my chest all the way home. She was badly malnourished, so when I got home my mom and I fed her bread in warm milk. It's all her little body could keep down. The vet estimated that she was four weeks old, she weighed in at seven pounds, and probably had some wolf in her. Now she's seven years old and seventy pounds. All of it fast, sinewy muscle, and besides me, my mom's best friend.

I had been on my developmental contract for almost a year when I received a call to go back to Stamford for the first ever Funkin' Dojo. It was a training camp run by Dory Funk Jr. and Tom Prichard, set up for signed and unsigned talent to show their skills. It was also a refresher course for guys the office felt needed it. The camp included myself, Rodney Blackbeard, Glenn Kulka, Kurggan, Ahmed Johnson, Tiger Ali Singh, Darren Drozdov, Mark Henry, Shawn Stasiak, Mark Mero, Taka Michinoku, Matt Bloom (A-Train), and, once again, the forever reappearing Sean Morley.

I knew Glenn, Rodney, and Sean going in, but Sean and I were more alike. We didn't drink, smoke, or do drugs. We were there for one thing: to impress the front office enough so they would put us on TV. Looking back, I think it was like a do-or-die situation. Impress or get lost. Sean wasn't signed but he had been working in Japan, Mexico, and Puerto Rico full-time. I had been signed for a year but had only worked two World Wrestling Federation matches, the first against Glenn in Ottawa, the night after Bret and Vince had their infamous Montreal incident, and the other being the next night against Jay in Cornwall, Ontario. So if I included the Bob Holly one I'd only had three matches under my belt. I felt I had something to prove, and so did Sean.

> **We were there for one thing: to impress the front office enough so they would put us on TV.**

The first day of camp was tough. Dory Funk Jr. is a former NWA World Champion and a legend in the wrestling business. He's a class act, but he and Tom Prichard were tough trainers, and they had us taking about a hundred bumps that first day. It seemed everyone else was getting discouraged, but Sean and I relished it. That night, while licking our wounds in the hot tub, we decided we were gonna bust our asses and give the company no choice but to put us on TV.

Day after day we were up by six A.M., breakfast by seven A.M., in the gym by nine A.M., and over to the studio after lunch for bumps galore. Not to brag, just straight fact, but Sean and I kicked ass. One day they paired us against Tiger Ali Singh and Ahmed Johnson, both of whom were already working on TV. To be honest, neither were good workers, but Sean and I knew we had our work cut out for us. It was another test, and you know what? We pulled it off and had a decent match with them. Bruce Prichard was there that day and he, Dory, and Tom pulled us aside. They told us we were the two from the class who were shining and it was time to get us on TV. They just needed to work out our characters.

At first our names were thrown around for the "New" Midnight Express. Anything "new" in wrestling is the kiss of death. Adorable Adam and Sensual Sean never saw the light of day and we dodged that bullet. Finally, after four months of dark (nontelevised) matches, Sean and I were told it was time to shape our characters and get started. I had no clue what to expect. I was still doing my running man schtick in dark matches with a young upstart named Matt Hardy. For some reason it still got cheap heat but it didn't exactly have career longevity written all over it.

Sean had started taping vignettes as Val Venis, a former-porn-star-turned-wrestler. I always based Sexton Hardcastle on that premise and thought I could do quite a bit with that character. Looking back,

After you sleep with every woman in the company, where do you go?

I'm glad I wasn't saddled with it. After you sleep with every woman in the company, where do you go? Instead of a porn star I became Edge. A tortured soul. That was it. I had no clue what the hell that meant, and I really don't think anyone else did either. My vignettes involved me running around the streets of New York beating people up (and no, they didn't ask for my ATM card). I went to a studio and recited poetry to play over the vignettes. It definitely wasn't me, and I felt uncomfortable doing it. After this my spoken poetry was left on the cutting room floor, and I wouldn't talk on TV for another year. Rumors abounded that I would become a deaf-mute wrestler. Talk about the final nail in the coffin before I even got started.

The vignettes looked cool but didn't explain much to the crowd, which I think was the point. The problem was it didn't explain much to me either. Most of my contact with the writers came through Vince Russo, who wanted me to be a "modern-day Jim Morrison." I thought, What do I do, wander aimlessly down the ramp and flash the crowd with my Lizard King? I think what he wanted was what Jeff Hardy was doing in his final days for WWE. That's great, but it's just not me. When all was said and done, I wanted to look like a wrestler with tights and all. I've always hated it when guys look like they walked in off the street and stumbled into a wrestling ring. The creative department drew up a character who had leather pants, green hair, a blue silk shirt, and some chains around his neck. I would have looked like a Bee Gee on crack!

I would have looked like a Bee Gee on crack!

Now that I said I was uncomfortable with poetry and wanted to wear wrestling gear, it was time to hash out the name. Russo came to the table with Riot and Rage. Once again, in my eyes, it didn't seem to fit. I'm the one who had to pull it off, so I wanted to be comfortable with it. Now here comes the birth of the name Edge. I wish it was some cool, outlandish story, but it isn't. As a matter of fact, just skip this part . . . okay, only joking. I was driving from Syracuse to Albany

Pants fabric as discussed with Adam Copeland & Vince Russo.

Please, let's all ignore the idea of me and green hair.

with Don (who was working as the Jackyl) throwing around some band names. Finally the name of the radio station we were listening to dawned on us. It was EDGE 10-something, and Don suggested, "How about 'Edge'?" Although I would have preferred Adam Copeland, it didn't seem like a bad alternative.

Even though I still had no clue who, or what, Edge was, I had at least talked everyone into letting me look like a wrestler. Who knew that with the inception of the Hardy Boyz and Raven that half the wrestling world would be wearing street pants or jean shorts. It worked for the Hardys, but my character is based on conquering the wrestling world, not a rave. Now everything was in place and it was time to make my debut.

Looking "tortured."

My World Wrestling Federation TV debut took place on a taped *Raw* from Austin, Texas. It didn't turn out too well. Actually, it sucked. Because I was a tortured soul I was told my entrance was to be through the crowd. Okeydoke. I wrestled and occasionally let out a primal scream. I was lost and it showed. My opponent for the debut was one of the Los Boricuas, Jose Estrada Jr. I had a feeling throughout the day that he wasn't cool with the fact that he was putting me over. Knowing what I do now, I know he wasn't cool with it. The finish was supposed to be my downward spiral, one-two-three, and a nice debut for Edge. Instead, I knocked Estrada out with a hilo to the floor. After Timmy White told me he was on dream street I was visibly shaken. I won by a countout and left back through the crowd with J.R. announcing what an inauspicious debut Edge had made. Wow, thanks for the morale booster. Just what I needed to hear at that point. Jose ended up with some pinched nerves in his neck, and eventually he came back for another short run with the company.

This destroyed the confidence I had built. Besides the occasional shiner, I had never hurt anyone. Now, in what was my first aired match, I knocked my opponent out. I called him weekly to see how he was, but I could just imagine what my perception was in the locker room.

I was lost and it showed.

From that point on I floated, but the office showed faith in me by choosing me to be Sable's mystery partner at *SummerSlam 1998*. Our opponents were Marc Mero and Jacqueline. Sable had no prior wrestling experience, so we all got together in Stamford to work on some things for the match. Sable had pulled off a top rope hurracanrana on Marc and they wanted to use it for the finish. I knew that this was my PPV debut, and I needed to be involved in the finish

Taking it to Marc Mero.

somehow. I pitched the tag finish Jay and I used to use. Sable would stand in front of me, roll backward, and I would catch her from behind around the waist, pick her up, and slam her down in a splash across Marc. It helped all of us, the match, and it was a cool move that always got a reaction. My first Madison Square Garden appearance was kind to me that night, and I had my first PPV behind me.

Life was good. I was finally on TV, and along the way I had stumbled upon the love of my life. I would wind up being wrong (once again), but hindsight is always 20/20. I just wish in this case my foresight could have been 20/20. C'est la vie.

It was the *Over the Edge* PPV in May 1998 in Milwaukee. Sean had told me he was bringing his sister to the show. That day Sean grabbed me and said "Ya gotta come meet my sister." I said okay, but I didn't see the big rush. I mean, I'm comfortable enough in my masculinity to admit that Sean's a good-looking guy, but he would make a very scary woman. I honestly couldn't remember his sister's name or what she looked like from our brief encounter five years before.

Sean led me to a seat in front of a good-looking blonde and announced that this was his sister Alanah. My, how she'd grown. There was an instant attraction and we hung out the entire trip. We started dating in June, which leads me to the somewhat disastrous story of our first date.

I would wind up being wrong. . . .

When we had first started dating I had yet to make my ill-fated TV debut. I was doing dark matches, and during one of them I executed a top rope legdrop. I felt discomfort right away but finished the match. When I got back to Canada I went to see my doctor. It seemed my ass bump had brought a cyst to the surface, directly on the end of my tailbone. I had to sit on one cheek. It sucked, and I haven't done that move since. I asked the doctor my options. He told me I had to have it cut out. I wasn't thrilled, but our first date was the next day, and my TV debut was looming the next week. I had to do something. Right there someone was trying to tell me what a huge pain in the ass this relationship would be in the future.

111

The doctor froze my ass and cut away. I think he went a little light on the freezing because I felt the incision, and it wasn't fun. After packing the wound it still wouldn't stop bleeding, so he struck me with the final, embarrassing blow. He told me I should wear a maxi pad for about a week, until the wound healed, to avoid having a bloody stain on the ass of my pants. So, yes, I had a *maxi pad on my ass* for my TV debut. Who the hell else can say that? I definitely came away from this with a new respect for women and their monthly visitor.

> I left the hospital walking like a penguin with a firecracker shoved up its ass and a maxi pad on my gluteus maximus.

So I left the hospital walking like a penguin with a firecracker shoved up its ass and a maxi pad on my gluteus maximus. Whew, I was ready for our first date. It was June 6, 1998, as I slowly sat myself down behind the wheel of my very bouncy 1988 Izuzu Trooper for the three-hour drive to Alanah's. I think I hit every bump on the way there and Maxi Pad Man arrived looking flushed and walking slowly. That night we went to Alanah's friend Tanya's apartment for dinner and a movie. Strange first date, but I didn't care. That, however, is when the real problems started.

Everyone has a weakness. Superman has kryptonite, I have a horrible allergy to cats. Tanya has two cats. It was going to be a long night. Next up was dinner. A dinner full of gastronomical food like chili, beans, and corn on the cob. I might as well have had an Ex-Lax milkshake to wash it down. After dinner we sat down (me very gingerly) to watch the movie. This is when the gas pains started and the night just got longer. Because of the cats I couldn't breath, I was breaking out in hives, and my eyes were red and itchy, I had a maxi pad on my ass, and now I seriously needed to pass wind. Scotty, please beam me the fuck up!

I was stuck in a small one-bedroom apartment with two virtual strangers, so I couldn't drop my gastral bombs without them smelling it. Talk about a shitty first impression! Like U2 so poignantly sang, I was stuck in a moment that I couldn't get out of. By the time the movie was done I was exhausted and in serious pain from holding my gas in, but Alanah said, "Why don't you stay the night, it's two A.M. and you're tired. We can sleep on Tanya's bed." We clung to opposite sides of the bed, fully clothed, and I didn't sleep a wink. Or so I thought. I was itchy, my ass hurt, and my stomach was killing me. Every guy reading this who has had to hold in gas on a first date knows where I'm coming from. Now multiply that times ten and you had my situation. Only about a year later did Alanah tell me my ass sounded like a French horn all night. I guess I fell asleep after all.

CHAPTER

My personal life was good, and I felt I had rebounded from my debut with my match at *SummerSlam*. I was now officially living my dream at the age of twenty-four. The ink was still drying on my brand-new five-year deal. No more developmental contract for me. I was the epitome of a happy young man.

That's not to say there still weren't some trials by fire. I had pulled the duty of wrestling the man monster known as Vader in his farewell match. Vader had a reputation for breaking people's backs. He's a six-four, four-hundred-fifty-pound bear of a man. The guy is a former WCW World Champion and a legend in Japan. Sometime during the day Bradshaw (John Layfield, or JBL), an Acolyte at the time, took me aside and said it might be a good idea to thank Vader for doing the favor for me before the match. I was thankful to get a win over Vader, so it seemed like the right thing to do. After I found and thanked Vader, Bradshaw pulled Vader aside and asked him, "Did he give you that, 'Thanks for doing the favor bullshit'?" Vader answered in the affirmative and Bradshaw proceeded to stir the shit. He's very good at that.

"Did he give you that thanks for doing the favor bullshit?"

Of course, everyone was gathered around the monitors backstage to see if this kid could pass the test Bradshaw had set up. It was a long walk through the back to the ring that night. It reminded me of my first WWE match with Bob Holly. Everyone tried to avoid eye contact with me as I stretched out before the match. They were all waiting to see if I'd get my head knocked off. Just like it happened against Bob when I walked through those curtains

They were all waiting to see if I'd get my head knocked off.

and heard the crowd, I was ready. Even though I had just witnessed Vader growling through his prematch routine at gorilla position (right behind the curtain to the arena, named after the legendary Gorilla Monsoon).

I can't fully explain the adrenaline rush I get as I make my way to the ring. At this point I still came through the crowd, but hearing their reactions makes you feel invincible. I've since changed my entrance, and thanks to advice from Michael Hayes, I realized that the more energy I give out on my entrance, the more I will get back. It's a beautiful relationship that I know I will sadly miss one day. With that kind of feeling, I didn't care what Vader had in store for me.

Hearing their reactions makes you feel invincible.

The match finally began and Vader started clubbing my head like Barry Bonds at a T-ball park. After the fifth or sixth shot (I lost count) I realized I had to fire back or get eaten alive—maybe literally. For every one of Vader's punches, I threw five stiff ones. Hey, at least I had quickness on my side. After that the big mastadon calmed down, and we worked the rest of the match. Very snug, but relatively safe.

After a downward spiral and the one-two-three I came to the back and thanked him again. Bradshaw was waiting like a hungry wolf to see if I would complain. Not me. Believe it or not, Jay hits harder with his punches that we've all deemed "the rubber mallets." So this wasn't so bad once I gauged Vader's bearlike paws.

This wasn't the first experience I had with the world of Bradshaw. Let me explain. The site was once again Copps Coliseum, and I was showering after having just worked Glenn Kulka in the opening match. I had yet to make my TV debut, but by now enough of the guys knew me, so I felt fairly comfortable. That is, until the light shining into the shower was suddenly blocked out. I looked over to see Bradshaw standing there in his full cowboy wrestling garb. In any other situation, a six-seven, three-hundred-pound man in chaps and a cowboy hat standing in the shower might be strange, but in this industry it's really not. So I went back to soaping myself up until I felt a large, calloused hand placed on my tush. I knew both of my hands were in front of me, and I had a sinking suspicion I knew what crazy Texan was lathering my ass (let me stress there was no insertion and no disappearing knuckles, if ya know what I mean). I turned to see Bradshaw's evil, ten-gallon-hat-topped grin, looked at Glenn (who was showering and avoiding eye contact nearby), and said, "He's actually soaping my ass!" At that point everyone listening outside the shower fell out laughing and ol' Adam was the butt end of another rib. Ahh, to be the new kid.

In a strange way, because of things like this, I knew Bradshaw liked me, and I was becoming one of the boys. It's his self-appointed job to test the guys coming in. Weed out the prima donnas. After working him in a dark match in Phoenix, Arizona, and not complaining about having my head clotheslined into the fourth row, I knew I'd passed the Bradshaw exam.

In the meantime, I had been mentioning Jay to anyone in the front office who would listen. Jim Cornette was a fan of Jay's work, so I pestered him. He got Jay a slot in the next Funkin' Dojo along with the Hardy Boyz, Test, and some guy named Kurt Angle. People used to ask me if I got Jay into the company. I didn't have the power to do that, but by pestering everyone just enough, I was able to open the door a crack, which he proceeded to kick wide open. They quickly signed him, and the two schoolboy chums were living their dream together.

My second PPV was *Breakdown* from, you guessed it, Hamilton's Copps Coliseum. My opponent was a guy who was on a short list of people I'd always wanted to work with, Owen Hart. I was very excited to work with Owen, and came to the table with quite a few ideas. We had a few hurdles to jump. Owen was working with a severely pulled groin. I was working on a minor groin pull, but I enjoyed every minute of that match. He later confided to me that our match was the last time he was looking forward to going out and having a "wrestling match." Pretty tough to beat that compliment. The finish of the match saw Jay make his World Wrestling Federation debut as Christian—a mysterious newcomer who cost me the match. From that point on we would forever be known as brothers to wrestling fans. To this day it's still the question I get asked the most: "Are you and Christian really brothers?" Let me set the record straight for good. We may act like brothers, and he is the closest thing I have to a brother, but we are not really brothers. I mean, I'm ugly, but not that ugly! Kurt has actually deemed Jay "the ugliest pretty boy in the world." I think the Creepy

I'm ugly, but not that ugly!

Little Bastard is actually proud of it. This brought on a strange situation that happened in Cornwall, Ontario, just a couple of years ago. Lance Storm, Jay, and I had stopped by a tiny family restaurant for our last meal before the show that night in Cornwall. The owner of the establishment came over to tell us proudly that our dad was in for meals all the time. Huh? I almost felt bad bursting this old fella's bubble. We went on to tell him that I never had a father, and that we were not really brothers. I guess someone decided it would be cool to claim Edge and Christian as his sons. Personally I don't understand it, but whatever floats your boat.

I almost felt bad bursting this old fella's bubble.

After the match with Owen, he and I went on to become good friends. If you were friends with Owen that meant plenty of ribs. I have to give an example of what Owen could be like in the ring. A couple of years down the road Jay and I were teaming against Owen and Jeff Jarrett for their tag team championships at a live event in Hershey, Pennsylvania.

Near the end of the match Jay and I got up in opposite corners for the dreaded ten punches, this time in unison. I noticed that Jeff, who I was punching, didn't seem to be selling the punches too well. I came down from the turnbuckles and found out why. Jeff and Owen had red foam clown noses on. While we had been punching them they had dug into their tights and placed them on their faces. We whipped them together and as they bumped the clown noses flew straight up into the air and landed on them. We laughed, they were in a heap laughing hysterically, and the crowd couldn't help but laugh, too.

Once we got comfortable with Owen and Jeff, the floodgates were opened. This was evidenced when we hit Oberhausen, Germany. It was a Tag Title match once again, and we'll pick it up as Owen and Jeff were getting some serious steam on yours truly. Suddenly Owen decided to throw serious out the window. He pulled a dastardly object out of his singlet . . . a napkin. Yep, you read that right. They both shot me into the ropes for a double clothesline with a napkin! Owen wrapped that napkin around his knuckles and blasted me with it. All behind the ref's back, of course. I sold the punch like I was out. I wouldn't get up, so Owen improvised and covered nothing but my knees. One-two, and I barely kicked out! That didn't work so he stuck his crotch in my face, forcing me to kick out before three. All the while he laughed like a hyena. He stood up and hid the napkin under his armpit. Our referee, Jim Korderas, called him on it. He raised his arms and the napkin floated harmlessly down to the mat.

Unhappily I was also involved in Owen's last match the night before he died. This night supplies me with great memories from a great man. He came to the ring with what looked like a bird's nest on top of his head. He'd actually just used gel and messed up his hair, causing it to stick out in all directions. He wore his blue-and-white Blue Blazer boots, his black-and-gold "I am not a nugget" T-shirt, and a silver, red, and black singlet. He was purposely trying to look like wrestling's Herb Tarlek of *WKRP* fame. I have a picture of Jay and me shooting Owen into the ropes doing his classic, old school high step, sound effects and all. During the comeback that night he ended up tangled in the ropes upside down on his head, his hair a mess and his eyes crossed as Jeff drawled in his southern accent, "My God, look at Owen, he's unbelievable." He truly was and I savor those memories. Many books and chapters have been dedicated to Owen and what you've read is true. Everyone I know speaks highly of the man, and that speaks volumes about the type of man he was, and the legacy he's left. Not too much time goes by that I don't think of Owen, and when I do, I smile. I think that's the way he would have wanted it.

After *Breakdown*, Jay (Christian) and I became two pieces of a puzzle. The third and final piece was Dave Heath, aka Gangrel. A pit bull of a wrestler who had a very cool vampire gimmick. The story line had Jay, my little "brother," brainwashed by Gangrel and the pair would face off against me. The battle lines had been drawn . . . until the writers decided to go down a different path.

The birth of the Brood: wrestling Gangrel on <u>Raw.</u>

On a subsequent episode of *Raw*, Gangrel was wrestling Kane. As he was on his way to being chokeslammed by the Big Red Machine, Christian made the save and a Big Red Beatdown ensued. As this happened I hit the ring to supposedly save the day. Instead I inexplicably joined in on the assault, and the Brood was born. No explanation was given to us, or the audience, but for the first time I felt comfortable in my World Wrestling Federation skin.

The Brood was a modern-day version of the movie *The Lost Boys*. Our music kicked ass (the New Jersey Devils still use it today). Our entrance, in my humble opinion, ranks up there with the coolest I've ever seen. The crowd quickly latched on to us. Brood merchandise was made and quickly sold. It felt like we were off and running. We all watched the movie *Blade* together and used the idea to "bloodbath" our opponents. It was a strange, but effective concept, and once again the fans dug it. We were supposed to be heels, but our audience didn't care. This was at a time when Stone Cold Steve Austin was on fire and the antihero was in.

Shortly thereafter we were inserted into Undertaker's Ministry of Darkness story line. A heel group based around Undertaker's new evil, occultlike persona. This led to our first appearance at a *WrestleMania*. It was *WrestleMania XV* from Philadelphia, and although we were not wrestling I was still excited to make an appearance. It also took place during a high-profile match. Undertaker was facing the Big Boss Man in a Hell in a Cell match. Our appearance involved the three of us being lowered to the cage from the rafters. Once we got there we would tear the cage open and drop a noose to 'Taker so he could "hang" Boss Man. It sounded like a good idea until we had to make our way up to the rafters at the top of the building. I don't have much of a problem with heights, but this was high, really high. The people below looked very tiny. We were put into harnesses that would be lowered by a motor. The match was well under way when we had to step backward off the rafter and let the harness catch. Not a good feeling. We hung there above the crowd in the rafters in antici-pation of our moment to strike. After what felt like a decade, it was time. We were slowly lowered down past the huge Philadelphia Flyers scoreboard, down to the cage. We clipped the harnesses to the cage and did our business. We clipped back into our harnesses and started to get raised back up to the rafters.

Everything was going fine until I came to a dead stop.

Everything was going fine until I came to a dead stop. Gangrel and Jay were already almost to the top but I was not moving. To make matters worse the cage was now being raised up toward my feet. I had nowhere to go. Boss Man was swinging by the noose in the cage and I was swinging above the cage still in full view of the crowd. As the cage got uncomfortably close my pulley was jerked upward—fast. Too fast. Apparently the motor had blown raising the three of us. The operators had fixed it but started to bring me up far too quickly. I was still swinging and now spinning toward the scoreboard. Luckily, I saw it coming and braced myself. I bounced off of it twice but I was finally clear and quickly heading for a showdown with the rafter that I was sure to lose. Thankfully, they slowed me down before I hit it and they pulled me back to safety. I got the hell out of there and have not been on a rafter since.

On paper, joining the Ministry looked like a great fit, but the fans continued to cheer us. It was hurting the heat the Ministry was trying to get, so they broke us away from the group. We worked a short angle with the other Ministry members, the Acolytes, Mideon, and Viscera. Four of the bigger guys on the roster, but the fans didn't care who we put over as long as they saw the flaming circle entrance,

"What the hell am I doing?"

bobbed to the music, and witnessed a bloodbath. We started encountering problems when injuries started to catch up to Gangrel. He was working with a torn pec. It looked like Tiger Woods had hit a drive off his chest. Because of this Jay and I took on most of the wrestling duties. Our confidence was really beginning to blossom, and, after much pestering, the writers finally gave us a chance to cut an in-ring promo.

Everyone was given a chance to talk except Jay. Someone obviously didn't think he was up to it. Of course, as you've seen over the last five years, they were wrong. Michael Hayes was our interviewer. He wore the most god-awful pastel yellow slacks and silk dress shirt combination I have ever seen. Michael asked Gangrel a question. He stammered his way to an answer. He was very uncomfortable with the microphone in his hand and it showed. Michael then asked Jay a question, which was returned with complete silence. Now, it was my turn. I had been mentally preparing a long time for my first shot at a promo. At this point I knew if I sucked we would not be talking for a very long time, and those deaf-mute rumors might start again. Vince Russo had given me some Shakespearean-like promo full of hath's and thou's. I didn't want to sound like Thor, so I came up with some ideas of my own. Reciting exactly what someone else has written sounds like you are doing just that.

I was very happy with my promo that night. It wasn't stupendous, but it wasn't horrible either. I came up with the final line, which I hoped could be our eventual tag line. "Beware, take care, because the freaks come out at night." After which the lights went out and a pastel yellow leisure suit was mercifully put out of its misery by a bloodbath. Little did I know that this promo would be the beginning of the end for the Brood.

"Beware, take care, because the freaks come out at night."

CHAPTER

Looking for revenge, Michael Hayes took on the managerial services of a new, up-and-coming tag team known as the Hardy Boyz, Matt & Jeff. Jay and I had worked with the Hardys a few times and found that we had great chemistry together. The Brood vs. Michael Hayes & the Hardy Boyz would be the beginning of a beautiful wrestling relationship that would help to revitalize tag team wrestling.

Near the beginning of the angle we worked a Six-Man Tag Team Elimination match on an episode of *Sunday Night Heat*. During the match I took a sling-shot DDT on the floor from Matt Hardy. We came down with a lot of force with my head breaking our fall. I was more or less knocked out. Matt rolled me in the ring and I managed to slur to

> *I woke up on a stretcher in a neck collar, felt my chipped teeth with my tongue . . . Not too much fun, but better than a broken neck.*

Jeff, "pin me." I rolled out of the ring, and that was it. I woke up on a stretcher in a neck collar, felt my chipped teeth with my tongue, and was told that I had probably gotten a stinger. Basically a compression of the disc that causes a burning sensation down your neck. Not too much fun, but better than a broken neck.

Throughout my childhood and early wrestling career I had sprained my neck three times. The first was my Spider-Man back flip from the coffee table. The second was during a Grade 6 cross-country track meet where I ran down a hill too fast, lost control, and took a flip bump on my skull. The third was a spinebuster from Jay (Christian) in London, Ontario, where it felt like I hit the mat at ninety miles an hour. So I guess you could say I have a history of neck problems. Despite the stinger, I didn't miss any time, and the feud with the Hardys raged on.

Outside the ring we were becoming even better friends with Matt and Jeff. We all felt like we were in the same position. We were all young guys with no history behind us, trying to do whatever we could in the ring to get the fans', and office's, attention. We started a little ritual that still lives on occasionally. We meet at various Outback Steakhouses across the country to eat and shoot the shit after the show. One particular night in Pittsburgh stands out from the rest.

Michael Hayes had literally taken the Hardys under his wing and rode from town to town with them. Michael didn't like to eat after the show, but he did like to drink. His poison of choice is Jack Daniel's, and on this night in Pittsburgh he'd had enough to challenge Gangrel to a headbutt contest. Now, call me crazy, but I had never witnessed one of these contests, so I was intrigued. We all filed out to the parking lot to watch this headbanging spectacle.

Michael started out the ceremonies with a head-cracking bang. However, he was quickly overwhelmed by Gangrel's large, granitelike cranium. Gangrel was advancing like a deranged fan moshing at a Slayer concert. Michael was backpedaling, but the Freebird in him wouldn't give up. They stood banging heads in the parking lot until the testosterone levels got too high, and the rest of us declared it a draw. Ahh, what big kids will do to amuse themselves.

On the work front it seemed like we were the only babyface team on the roster. We worked DX, D.O.A., the Acolytes, LOD 2000, the Nation of Domination, and of course our perennial foes, the Hardys. Our matches with the Hardys were really tearing it up on live events. Everything was rolling along great in the Brood camp until one day in Nashville, Tennessee. Gangrel, Jay, and I were standing around, admiring our brand-new T-shirt, being sold that night for the very first time. We were unsuspecting when Terry Taylor, one of our agents at the time, walked up, pointed at me, and said "babyface." He pointed at Gangrel and said "heel." What? This is the way we were told they were breaking up the Brood. I guess it was decided I could make it on my own. Jay was left in limbo while it was determined if I could make it on my own.

Gangrel and I had a tag team match that night on *Heat* against the Corporate Ministry (brutal group name by the way, I had to get that off my chest). At the end of the match when we seemingly had everything under control, Gangrel turned on me. One Impaler DDT later, and that was it. According to the story line he was jealous of my popularity. The following week on *Raw* from Louisville, Kentucky, Gangrel and I wrestled to a no-contest after he pushed me down the fiery pit used in our entrance. Earlier in the day I was told the finish, so in my infinite wisdom (yes, that's my tongue firmly planted in cheek, again), I decided Gangrel should backdrop me down this small fiery square. Our agent Gerry Brisco quickly vetoed that one, so I suggested a hip toss. Still stupid and risky, but I felt like I needed to make an impression. Gerry wanted to practice it once, complete with fire, just to make sure I could pull it off. It's hard to fathom that I would willingly be thrown down a fiery hole cut into a steel stage by a crazed-looking "vampire" during the middle of the day in Louisville, just for a dry run. Please allow a moment for this to sink in . . . okay, let's move on to my first attempt. With no crowd or adrenaline, it was tough to charge and try to take his hip toss, but I did it. I bounced off the steel lip of the hole and did my best impression of a human slinky to the ground five feet below. Hey, at least I missed the fire, but it still fuckin' hurt, so Gerry didn't need to veto that one, I did.

With no crowd or adrenaline, it was tough to charge and try to take his hip toss, but I did it.

We finally came down to a decision, and now it was match time. Wrestling Gangrel was like fighting a pit bull. Matt Hardy dubbed him "the wild animal," and it stuck. That night we fought fang and nail. (Get it? Fang and nail, he's a vampire . . . ahh screw you, I like it.) It was decided that Gangrel should just push me down to the fiery depths of hell, or the arena floor, but that doesn't sound quite as dramatic. I was six-five going down a four-foot-square hole, but thankfully my head cleared the steel stage and I survived the landing, in an eye-clenched, fetal position on the crash mat below.

That night we fought fang and nail.

The next week on *Raw*, Gangrel and I were booked in the first, and I believe last ever, Bloodbath match. Jay had been inconspicuous in a two-week TV absence. A bucket of "blood" was placed at ringside. (We couldn't get a cauldron? C'mon.) The loser would be doused with this supposed plasma. That night the wild animal and I beat the hell out of each other. The end of the match came when Gangrel rolled out of the ring to get the bucket. The Bloodbath lights and music came on, followed by the houselights being cut; it was pitch black. When the lights came back on, Gangrel lay in a heap, covered in the "viscous fluid," with Jay standing over top of him. My little brother had seen the light and saved me like a damsel in distress! I was declared the winner and Jay came in the ring for a short staredown, and eventual hug from his "big bro." I remember Vince wasn't exactly happy with our brotherly embrace, but usually we want to fight each other, not hug, so it was a little forced. I guess it was decided I wasn't quite ready to make it on my own, and I wasn't. So the gothic, babyface tag team of Edge & Christian was officially born.

Here I am in the Canadian national costume, the hometown hockey jersey.

You can see how much I loved
being with my grandparents.

My mom, Judy. I'm seven here. COURTESY OF THE COPELAND FAMILY.

Here's the obligatory playing-hockey photo.
COURTESY OF THE COPELAND FAMILY.

Showing off my
best move to Jay.

Here we are: Jay and I, professional wrestlers. This is an early shot of the Suicide Blondes in Windsor, Ontario.

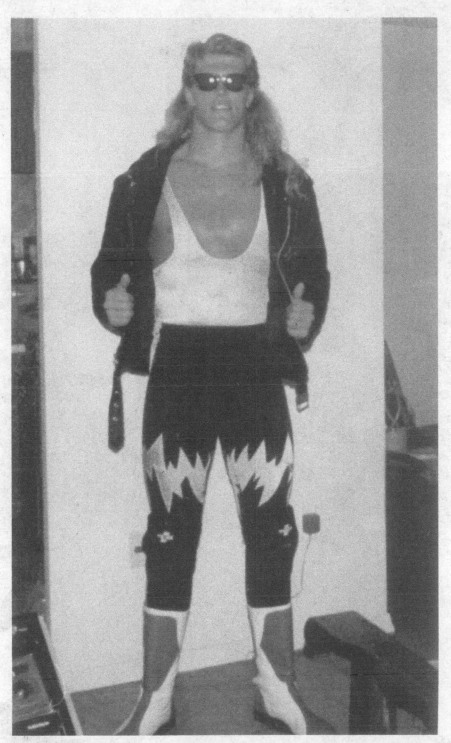

My first wrestling gear. Fear the mullet! COURTESY OF THE COPELAND FAMILY.

Thug Life: Joe Hitchen (now Legend), Jay, me, Rhyno, and "Handsome" Johnny Bradford.

Survivor Series 2001. I took the I-C title from Test.
I kept thinking about our first match in Bret's poolroom.

With my mom in a hotel room in Houston just before <u>WrestleMania X-Seven</u>.

The start of a very long and successful feud
with Kurt Angle, at <u>King of the Ring</u>.

The beginning of my feud with Christian (Jay).
It hurts just looking at this photo.

That little puppy I saved. Taking Frisco for a walk.
COURTESY OF THE COPELAND FAMILY.

Now, that's the proper way to contain YZↃ.

It feels great
to be back.

Taking down Randy Orton.

On live events Jay (Christian—Beware: Edge Rant! For those of you faithful readers tired of seeing the parenthesis around "Jay" or "Christian," raise your hands. Okay, so obviously I'm not the only one, but my editor assures me that it's a necessary evil. So take out your frustrations on Simon & Schuster by burning this book. Obviously, this means you'll have to buy another one, which, of course, would not be an ulterior motive on my part!) and I found ourselves matched up against the Acolytes again. Bradshaw and Ron Simmons are two big, tough bastards, and while it was a clash in styles, it still worked. On TV I was being set in line for a match with Jeff Jarrett and a shot at the Intercontinental title at the *Fully Loaded* PPV in Buffalo, New York. Now, growing up, I'd always wanted the I-C—Intercontinental—title. It was the springboard, the stepping-stone to the World title. Some of my main influences growing up—Mr. Perfect, Randy Savage, Ricky Steamboat, Shawn Michaels, and Bret Hart—had all excelled with it. I was never told much creatively in advance, but somehow I just knew I wouldn't be taking the title home with me. Due to a very unexpected scenario, I was proven wrong once again.

The night before the PPV on June 24, 1999, we had a live event. That's one thing people don't always realize. We don't just perform on TV. We work about 220 to 250 times a year, more often than not untelevised. This show took place at the SkyDome in Toronto—forty minutes from my front door. It was the same building where I witnessed *WrestleMania IV*. The Dome was set up tent fashion, so we had about 25,000 in attendance that night. Once again, Jay and I were scheduled to take on the Acolytes in the first match. They put the hometown boys over and we headed back to the showers. Our work was done. Or at least until Pat Patterson, one of our agents and a wrestling genius, rushed up to inform me that I'd be wrestling Jeff Jarrett in the fourth match. It was advertised as Jeff vs. Ken Shamrock for the I-C title. The problem was that Shamrock was stuck in Detroit, and I was his replacement.

Pat came up with "an 'ell of an idea" (French-Canadian accent for ya, he mixes his H's. I'm Hedge, Hunter is Unter). I would win the match but not the title because I was not the contracted opponent. Cool. Jeff was in the ring when it was announced Ken would not be there. Jeff grabbed his title belt and went to leave but "You Think You Know Me," the opening strands of my music, filled the cavernous building.

I hit the ring like a gunshot. The match was on, and Jeff and I did our thing. Here comes the spear, the finish, the place goes apeshit! The problem arose when referee Earl Hebner handed the title back to Jeff and my hometown peeps were none too pleased. The announcement was made by Howard Finkel, and that just added fuel to the fire.

"Go get your belt, Champ." Huh? Say What?

At this point our other agent, grizzled veteran Jack Lanza, came down to the ring with a gleam in his eye and a bounce in his step. (I'm embellishing. I'm allowed. It's my story.) He asked Earl to find out from Jeff what our finish was the next day. It was relayed back that Jeff was indeed going over (at this point I was not privy to this type of information). I was standing beside Jack and Howard on the floor and I could tell Jack's wheels were turning until he looked at me and said, "Go get your belt, Champ." Huh? Say What? "Go get your belt, Champ." Are you serious? "Go get it." All of this was filmed for the huge Jumbotron at the Dome, and I later got my hands on a copy. It's hilarious because you can actually hear this verbal exchange take place.

So Earl hadn't screwed another Canadian in Canada and I went to grab my title. The official announcement was made. I'd grown up hearing Howard announce, "And the new Intercontinental Champion . . . ," but it means so much more when he announces your name at the end of that sentence. It was amazing. I literally could not believe it because it was not supposed to happen. Jack called an

Losing my first I-C title.

audible, and I have to admit, he was right, although Jeff wasn't too happy. The crowd and I got an unexpected surprise.

The next day the *Toronto Sun* had a full-page photo, and the look on my face is priceless. My smile was so big, my teeth looked like white tombstones! It was a definite goose-bump moment. It was my first WWE title, and not knowing I'd win it made it even more special. I only held the title for one day (no change of plan there), but even having it for such a short period meant so much to me. Little did I know I'd win it three more times (and counting?). The match at *Fully Loaded* went well. When he wanted us to, Jeff and I always clicked in the ring. Deborah was at Jeff's side and Gangrel did a run in to help Jeff win the title back. It was my first real opportunity to show what I could do on my own with a title involved. After my brief brush with the I-C title, some serious changes took place in my life.

It wasn't better in the Bahamas.

One day, while running errands in Toronto, I received a very intriguing phone call. The call was from the president of a production company based in Toronto. He wanted me to come by their offices; to make me what he promised was an interesting offer. I decided to give it a shot, and the next day I went down to his building. I have to admit I was impressed because his setup kicked some serious ass. I was brought into a plush loft-style office and the pitch was made. He wanted to base a TV show around me! Okay, very interesting, that much was true. He had a script for two shows and wanted to know which one I was interested in and it was mine. They were both based on comic books so he peaked my interest even more. One had me playing the lead role of a spy, the other a classic hero who has a monstrous side à la the Incredible Hulk. He told me the budget his company was willing to put behind it, and once again it was impressive. Supposedly, billboards across North America would have my face splashed all over them and he would make me a star. The company had an impressive track record so I took him at his word. He also promised I could choose the shooting location of the series. If I wanted Toronto, it would be Toronto. He offered me a nice salary and the offer was becoming more tempting, but there had to be a hitch, right? Yep, I'd have to quit wrestling.

Okay, so let's summarize. I could work at home and sleep in my own bed every night. I could make a comparable if not better salary and supposedly become a star. No more grueling travel schedules. No more punishment to my body. On paper it sounds like

I could work at home and sleep in my own bed every night. I could make a comparable if not better salary and supposedly become a star . . . On paper it sounds like a no-brainer . . .

a no-brainer, but in my head, and more important in my heart, it was a different story, and my decision was made the minute he told me I would have to quit wrestling. The answer was no. It was impossible to juggle both full-time (as The Rock has now proven) and leaving wrestling was, and is, not an option. Most people reading this might not be able to understand this train of thought, but I have not regretted my decision once.

Wrestling is what I do.

Fresh off of this decision, I made another huge one. I decided to propose to Alanah. We had been together for a year and it felt like the right thing to do. I proposed during the Wrestle Vessel. A cruise that took fans and wrestlers to Nassau in the Bahamas. She said yes, and we finalized plans to actually move to Paradise Island, Bahamas, shortly thereafter. I signed a yearlong lease and we were Bahamas bound for at least a year. After a very annoying day of flights we managed to lug all of our belongings into our new town house/condo. It was a beautiful complex that was completely empty except for our neighbors, Sean and his girlfriend, Lourdes.

I had one day to relax before I had to fly out for my next tour. This is when the reality of my new situation began to set in. Travel was going to suck a big hard one every week. It was a West Coast swing

Travel was going to suck a big hard one every week.

and it took a full day of flights and three connections to get to L.A. Not fun, and I had a year of this travel to look forward to. I think my decision to leave after the year lease was up was made that first travel day. That feeling was reaffirmed two nights later as I turned on the news to see a hurricane the size of Texas heading directly toward Nassau and Paradise Island. By the time I called, the phone lines were already down and the airport was closed. I'm a hockey-watchin', snow-lovin' Canadian, so hurricanes were a new phenomenon to deal with. And I didn't deal well. I managed to get through my matches and the tour, after which I had to fly to Canada and wait for the Nassau airport to reopen. Finally, after two days, I made it home. Alanah was shaken but fine, as was the new home. I was back on the road the next day feeling my debut in the Bahamas had gone about as well as my TV debut.

This wouldn't be my last hurricane experience, but we'll get to that in a minute.

On the professional front Jay and I kept our gothic babyface team going, while the Hardys had dumped the headbuttin' Michael Hayes and the creative team paired them with Gangrel to form the New Brood. Matt, Jeff, Jay, and I talked about doing a best of seven series like Booker T and Chris Benoit for the WCW TV title, and Magnum T.A. and Nikita Koloff for the U.S. title. The difference was that we wanted every match to be a gimmick match. Texas Tornado, Cage, No Disqualification, Falls Count Anywhere, all leading to the grand finale and tie breaker, the first ever Tag Team Ladder match. We just needed something to climb for. We went to Vince Russo with the idea and he loved it, although the idea for every match to have a stipulation was thrown aside. Terri Runnels would be inserted in the story line, offering her managerial services and $100,000 to the winner of the T.I.T. . . . the Terri Invitational Tournament. Real clever, huh? The final match would be the Ladder match with the "sack o' money" hanging above us. To win, just climb the ladder and pull down the money. That would end up being easier said than done, and leads to my other hurricane experience.

We had never participated in a Ladder match before, so it had been arranged for us to meet in Stamford a day before the *No Mercy* PPV and go over some things. We felt like we had a lot to live up to from watching Shawn Michaels's perfect Ladder match, and we wanted to pull it off. The rest of the guys arrived right on schedule. I wouldn't be quite so lucky. I knew how important this match was to my career, so I brought Alanah along for the trip. Maybe we just had bad hurricane karma, but we got stranded in Miami due to a hurricane. Everything was flooded and shut down. The PPV was the next day in Cleveland. While I sat and watched the storm rage, the guys got the match together. One problem solved, now the fourth participant, me, had to find a way to get to Cleveland. I waited all night but the hurricane just would not quit. I made a last-ditch plane at six the morning of the show. I called the airline to see if the Tampa airport was open. It was. The hurricane was heading that way but hadn't stopped flights yet. There was a ten A.M. connection to Cleveland and

I booked us on it. We hopped in the car by six-thirty. I put on my Metallica . . . *And Justice for All* CD and drove a hundred miles an hour through a hurricane. It may sound impossible, but trust me, it isn't. The drive from Miami to Tampa takes three and half to four hours in good weather. I did it in three.

Soaked with sweat, we boarded the flight. Because of the connection, I wouldn't get to the Gund Arena until four P.M. Three hours before the biggest match of my life. I raced in to find the guys huddled in a hallway (now deemed our hallowed hall) going over the match. They had the skeleton of the match together but had been told to come up with three different finishes. One with Jay and I going over. Another with Jay turning on me, and finally one with the Hardys going over. As you all probably know by now, the last scenario was the final decision.

Originally, we were supposed to go over and start a program with the Mean Street Posse, Shane McMahon's childhood friends, and great guys, but not the best wrestlers in the world. Terri would be the mastermind and have the Posse waiting to attack us at the bank as we cashed our $100,000 check. Once again this was a Russo idea. The goths vs. the jocks. Not the best idea I'd ever heard, but not the worst either, and, like I said, we liked the Posse and thought it might be possible to pull a good match out of them. Finally it was decided the Hardys needed the win more. They were the newer team and less established at that point. Jay and I were disappointed, but we all knew that with what we had planned it didn't matter who won. We were ready to make history.

> **We all knew that with what we had planned it didn't matter who won. We were ready to make history.**

The first ever Tag Team Ladder match turned into a scenario where everyone wins. The company, all four of us, and the fans. Because it was the first of its kind we had a clean canvas on which to paint a wrestling masterpiece, and that's exactly what we did. Mick Foley and Shawn Michaels paved the way for our risk-taking ways, and I feel all four of us (and eventually the Dudleyz) are partially responsible for all of the stupid risks taken in our industry over the last few years. But I still wouldn't change a thing, and let's face it, we were four young studs eager to impress and trying to make our mark. Some people can do it posing, some people can do it drinkin' beer, kickin' ass, and talkin' trash. We felt we needed to be daredevils.

The crowd that night in Cleveland had no clue what to expect. Chyna had just become the first woman to capture the I-C title in a Good-Housekeeping match, but we were going to leave that match in the dust. The audience knew something big was brewing, they just didn't know when it would explode. Early in the match I was shooting Matt into the ropes. Jay was shooting Jeff in at the same time. Jeff hit the ropes first so the ropes were open more than usual. This caused Matt to go through the ropes and come back, causing his face to ricochet off the top rope. He recovered, but I could feel some panic starting to take hold, so I told them to slow it down, there was no rush. After that they settled in, and we got ready to make some jaws drop.

After Gangrel got tossed from ringside by our referee Timmy White, the fireworks began. Jay rammed Jeff into a corner with a ladder, ran

> *We were four young studs eager to impress . . . Some people can do it posing, some people can do it drinkin' beer, kickin' ass, and talkin' trash.*

up it, and dropkicked the trapped Hardy, setting the tone. From there the shit was on! A Jeff Hardy leg drop onto a ladder caused a seesaw effect that legitimately almost knocked Jay and Matt out. Downward spirals, hip tosses, neckbreakers—you name it, we did it, from way up high, and unknowingly we started a dangerous trend in sports entertainment. Ladder matches became a little too popular after this, eventually leading to another first that we were involved in, the TLC match (tables, ladders, and chairs to the uninformed, but we'll get to that ugly beast later).

Jeff has a wacky, eccentric, creative mind and he came up with a great finish. All four of us were fighting on ladders placed underneath the sack. Jeff had knocked Jay off their ladder while I pushed Matt off of ours. He bounced off the ropes and into Jeff's ladder. As the ladder fell, Jeff stepped off onto mine, where Matt had just been, and knocked me off as I reached for the money. It went without a hitch until Jeff had to yank the sack down and fell twelve feet to the mat in a heap, taking what might have been the ugliest bump of the match.

> The crowd was standing, too, giving us a standing ovation. I didn't expect that reaction and it actually choked me up.

By the end of this match the Hardys were bona fide fan favorites. As Jay and I collected ourselves, we stood up and looked around. The crowd was standing, too, giving us a standing ovation. I didn't expect that reaction and it actually choked me up. I'll never forget that moment. We made our exit back through the crowd and headed to the dressing rooms, where everyone there stood up and applauded. To get that respect from your peers is a special thing. We found the Hardys, toasted each other with a beer (Matt and Jeff's first), hugged, and cemented a bond that exists to this day. Shortly afterward, Mick Foley came up to the four of us and congratulated us on securing a spot within the company. He didn't have to go out of his way to do that, and it meant a lot to all of us.

The next day we were licking our wounds and found out we had the night off. Just a nonphysical promo segment with the Hardys. Little did any of us know how special this promo would end up being to all of us. The Hardys went to the ring first and declared that they were

Huh? What's going on? Is Stone Cold on his way down?

Matt and Jeff Hardy. The Hardy Boyz, not the New Brood. Cue up "You Think You Know Me," and Jay and I were on our way to the ring. We got in the ring and stood face-to-face, and once again the crowd, this time at Penn State, came to their feet. Huh? What's going on? Is Stone Cold on his way down? What was happening was another standing ovation. I was overwhelmed. All of our hearts were in our throats and on our sleeves (sounds difficult and painful, but it happened). So I took this unexpected opportunity and said, "Last night the crowd gave us a standing ovation, and tonight this crowd is giving us a standing ovation because we all busted our asses. Guys, I'm shootin' here, it was an honor." At that Jay and I extended our hands and we all shook. It was a really great moment for us. According to story line, E&C and the Hardys were on the same page and became friends on TV. It was the first and last time, and it was short-lived. We teamed together at the *Survivor Series* to take on the Hollys and Too Cool, only to start feuding again after. Let's face it, we made much better enemies.

O ne day, shortly after this match, I was sitting at home when I received a phone call from Lynn Brent in our talent relations department. She asked me if I wanted a part in the new *Highlander* movie being shot in Romania. My part would take eight days to film and I'd miss four shows. I had passed on this type of opportunity once already, and besides, it was only eight days, so I agreed to do it.

I flew into Bucharest, Romania, and quickly got hit with culture shock. Romania had recently come out of communism and it was still reeling from the effects. Many of the buildings were half finished because the communist dictator was overthrown and assassinated. I ended up learning how to use a sword in this huge but only partial-ly finished parliament building.

My character in the movie was named Lachlan. The leader of a band of Irish thugs who preyed on the rich who happened to pass

through their forest. Of course, my scene involved fighting, and also some swordplay. I had two days to learn sword work. Two days to learn how not to hurt these tiny actors. Luckily for them the swords were blunted and we choreographed our fight scene tighter than a Lucha Libre match.

I had two days to learn sword work. Two days to learn how not to hurt these tiny actors. Luckily for them the swords were blunted . . .

Finally it was time to shoot. With the moon still full, we would drive out to a Romanian forest at five A.M. There were wild dogs howling until the sun came up. That became even more fitting when I found out that we were filming in the forest where Vlad the Impaler was supposedly beheaded! The place definitely had atmosphere.

We shot my scene in December. It was supposed to take place in seventeenth-century Ireland, so our attire had to capture the time. It was bitterly cold, and the clothes were not warm. My wardrobe consisted of wool pants, knee-high suede boots, and a *Seinfeld* (or Gangrel)-like puffy shirt. I quickly realized that a Romanian forest in December is not the place to wear seventeenth-century clothing. I also quickly realized why wrestling is my first love. On movie sets you hurry up to wait, shoot the same scene fifty times, and don't eat enough. I think you could hear my stomach growling on the audio. Wrestling is one take. Take it or leave it. It adds a sense of urgency and gives you an immediate reaction. Between all the waiting and the Romanian elements, it definitely put me in the mood for a sword fight. I'll never forget the look of fear on Christopher Lambert's face as I charged, with full wrestling intensity and sword held high. He was very diminutive and he looked like he was about to piss his pants. In hindsight it actually might have warmed him up, but I went easy on him. I must have sucked at acting

I'll never forget the look of fear on Christopher Lambert's face . . . He looked like he was about to piss his pants.

because my lines were almost nonexistent in the final cut. They also had to rerecord my lines at a sound stage in New York a few months later. They had used some cheap, but ancient, Romanian audio equipment. In the final cut my scene definitely has that delayed-dialogue, kung fu–movie feel to it.

Even though my part was almost nonexistent, for some reason I ended up doing most of the publicity for the movie. I made an appearance on *The View*. Yes, the show that has middle-aged women (and Barbara Walters) sitting around a coffee table drinking some java. Lisa Ling was by far the coolest on the show and we taped a pretty amusing and somewhat painful segment before the program. The producers laid a mattress on the floor and wanted Lisa to hip toss me onto it, which would showcase my athletic ability and extraordinary grappling prowess. To illustrate how untrue the above statement is, I overshot the mattress and took a hip toss from Lisa Ling on the wooden floor. It sounded like a gunshot and everyone panicked. Of course, being the supposedly tough hombre that I am, I hopped up like nothing had happened even though my back was on fire and my right hand was numb for a day from breaking my fall. All in the name of Entertainment!

> The movie experience was fun, and I'd do it again, but it made me realize even more that wrestling is my calling.

I also did *TRL* on MTV with some host named K.K. something. I guess Carson Daly had the day off. I came out in full E&C valley boy mode wearing board shorts, a T-shirt, and sandals. Not exactly the best choice, but that's me. I also got the host's name wrong (on purpose) and introduced a Bon Jovi video. The movie experience was fun, and I'd do it again, but it made me realize even more that wrestling is my calling.

CHAPTER

After my cinematic experience I went back home. Home to a wrestling ring with the Hardys once again on the opposite side. They had just finished the first ever Tag Team table match versus the Dudleyz in Madison Square Garden at the *Royal Rumble.* Two days later, on January 25, 2000, we found ourselves stuck in Baltimore because of the **BLIZZARD OF THE CENTURY** (trust me it deserves caps). Our *SmackDown!* taping that night was postponed to the twenty-seventh, which meant we went live on Thursday. This left a bunch of bored wrestlers with nothing to do for two days. For the most part, wrestlers are just a bunch of big kids. Hey, we jump around in tights for a living, what do you expect? So when big kids are bored for two days, strange things can happen. This next story is one of those instances.

The Hardys were staying at the Microtel. An illustrious establishment with rooms the size of a microwave oven. I was staying at the same hotel as Jay and Chris Jericho; the Marriot down the street. The three of

When big kids are bored for two days, strange things can happen.

us decided to hit the restaurant in the hotel. We also decided to order three bottles of girlie wine and proceeded to get drunk. The ol' white zinfandel hit us pretty quick and we decided it was too early to call it a night. We called the Hardys, who were having a little get-together of their own that included Lita, Joey Abs from the Mean Street Posse, and their buddies Joey Matthews and Christian York. Apparently the white z had reared its sweet, fruity head in their room, too, because when we got there Matt was applying all of our finishing holds to Lita (in a nice way, of course).

I sat down over by the window with Jeff to watch this comedy unfold. Lita almost made Jericho tap, and Jay would randomly throw cheap shots just like he does in the ring. After a little while the room felt like a sauna, so we took the screen off the window. Maybe it was

Maybe it was that sweet nectar talking, but as I looked out the window at the snow below, I decided I needed to be in it.

that sweet nectar talking, but as I looked out the window at the snow below, I decided I needed to be in it. I looked at Jeff and said, "If I jump, will you?" Once again that big-kid theory comes into play. He said sure, and I leaped like a clumsy lion out the second-story window. I still don't really know why, and I wouldn't advise it, but it was damn fun! I landed in about three feet of snow and pulled myself out to see Jeff looking down incredulously. Do you remember when Wile E. Coyote would fall off the cliff and leave a perfect outline in the cement road below as the Roadrunner beep-beeped by? Well, I left a perfect Superfly splash impression in the snow, according to Jeff. It didn't take too long for everyone else to join in. Jeff swantonned next. Followed by Chris, Matt, Jay, and the rest. Now we were wrestling in snowbanks half-clothed in the Microtel parking lot. Jay ended up losing his brand-new bracelet that his girlfriend Denise had just bought him. He got a replica made that we titled "the mimicker." Denise knew the whole time that it was a phony, but she didn't bust him on it until about two years later. (Jay, what a dumb ass.) Anyway, we probably gave the night attendant at the hotel a heart attack. Imagine six sweaty, wet, snow-covered, half-naked wrestlers piling through your lobby at two A.M. Like I said, big kids with too much time on their hands.

In between our offbeat, out-of-the-ring shenanigans, E&C inserted themselves into the Dudleyz/Hardys angle. It ended up making for a potent, volatile mix. Jay and I had a match at *No Way Out* from Hartford, Connecticut, against the Hardys to determine the number one contenders to the Tag Team titles. That same night the Dudleyz had defeated DX and were crowned the new champions. They had come over from ECW and had eventually hit their groove. They were putting eighty-year-old Mae Young through tables, and they were red hot. The winner of our match got them at *WrestleMania XVI* at the Pond in Anaheim, California. During our match the Hardys were the crowd favorites but we still wrestled a double babyface match. In the end, Terri turned on Matt and Jeff and it cost them the match, to our confusion. This ended up being the subtle beginning to our heel turn.

In the weeks leading to *WrestleMania* the story line teased Terri coming between Jay and me to do an eventual singles feud. It

I gave her my "nice spear but it still looked like it killed her."

had been decided that after *'Mania,* Jay and I would finally split and do our singles program. I would stay babyface and Jay would join forces with Terri to form an evil duo. Jay and I spoke up and said we didn't want to do it, at least not yet. We were both concerned because we felt that we had only scratched the surface of what we could do as a tag team. On a *SmackDown!* from Long Island we refused Terri's management offer. She slapped me, and I speared her. I was really worried I'd tear her little body in two. I was tentative, but she was a trooper. I gave her my "nice spear but it still looked like it killed her." Thankfully she was okay.

Meanwhile, the Hardys had been thrown into the tag match at *WrestleMania.* It would be another first. The first ever Triangle Ladder match. In the weeks leading to the PPV, the Hardys were the definite babyfaces. The Dudleyz were slowly turning face. We were slowly turning heel, and liking it. It was a natural fit for us, and was essentially the baby steps of what we would later deem the E&C Dynasty. As you can see, modesty was not our team policy.

Two scary moments came on *SmackDown!* in the weeks leading to *WrestleMania.* The first happened in Baltimore and it didn't involve jumping out of a second-story window. Instead, I found myself lying on a table set up on the arena floor. The Dudleyz were about to get some wood at the expense of the ol' Edgemeister. D-Von picked Jay up for a powerbomb in the ring and handed him off to Bubba, who was standing above me on the apron. Bubba turned and drove Jay through me and through the table. I looked up to protect Jay in case he was falling short. When I did, I caught his knobby elbow right in the mush. I lay in a heap, my bottom lip shredded (I needed twelve stitches), trying to pull my four top front teeth back into place. I was taken to the hospital where a brace was put on to hold my teeth in place. I went to my dentist in Toronto, who drilled out my front teeth and jammed metal rods in them. Not fun, but at least I still have my real teeth. The second scare came weeks later after we had attacked the Hardys and set up ladders from which we would dive onto them. Enter the Dudleyz. Bubba had never pushed a ladder before. You see, the key is to guide the ladder and let the poor fool (in this case me) take his own bump. Well, Bubba pie-faced that ladder like it owed him money. One second I was standing on top of the ladder. The next it was closed, and I fell from the top, folding around it ribs first. I was sure I had broken my ribs, but luckily I was fine. We definitely needed a ladder-pushing lesson before the next match.

Jay and I had done some frustrated, heelish, and humorous commentary leading into *WrestleMania,* and I think it saved us as a team. Vince, or anyone else for that matter, didn't know if we had it in us. He knew now, and he liked what he was hearing. The original plan was for the Hardys to take the titles and Jay to once again turn on me. Because our heel schtick was striking a chord it was decided that we were going to go over and claim our first WWE Tag Team Championships! Besides, at that point, like I'd heard somewhere before, we needed the win more.

For all of the six participants in the first ever Triangle Ladder match, it would be our first wrestling appearance at a *WrestleMania*. Vince gave us the "spectacular but safe" speech, which we would hear many times over the years. We put some intense pressure on ourselves to steal the show. It was one of the featured matches at *WrestleMania XVI*. Tag team wrestling was important again and we were proud to be spear-heading it.

We all sat down with Michael Hayes and Tom Prichard to set up the match. I don't usually like to set up too much in advance. It's better to feel the crowd and make it more spontaneous. However, in these matches, it became a necessary evil to set everything up. It was supposed to be the first ever Triangle Ladder match, but basically it turned into the first TLC—table, ladder, chair—match, just without that title.

We wanted to make sure everyone came out of the match strong because we would end up doing business together for a long time (almost two years when all was said and done). There were so many memorable moments that took place in this match. Christian's dive to the floor off the ladders. Jeff's helacious swanton from the top of a twelve-foot ladder, through a table, to the floor. The table and ladder

> **It was like the dream sequence from _Wayne's World_ except "Dream Weaver" wasn't playing.**

platform that I pushed Matt off of, into a sick-looking flip-bump through a table below. This was the part of the war that stands out to me most of all. It was like the dream sequence from *Wayne's World* except "Dream Weaver" wasn't playing. It was all fuzzy around the edges of my vision. Either that or I was on the verge of unconscious-ness. I reached up on this very wobbly table set on top of two ladders and snatched those titles for the very first time! Finally we had done it!

We went from being little boys playing in Jay's side yard on a mattress with cardboard tag team belts, to being big boys

Wrestling is a weird creature.

holding the real thing fifteen feet above a packed house at the Pond. We also did what we set out to do, and that was steal the show. When we came to the back we found the Hards and the Duds and had a group hug. Wrestling is a weird creature. We had just finished knocking the shit out of each other and now the six of us stood hugging in a hallway. But it was a special moment for all of us. We had all helped to elevate one another and to start carrying the torch for a new era in tag team wrestling. It was integral to the show again like the glory years of The Hart Foundation, the Rockers, the British Bulldogs, the Road Warriors, Demolition, and the Brain Busters, only with a brutal, violent, and modern twist.

We welcomed the Dudleyz into our ladder gang with open arms. The six of us had shared something that no one could take away. I don't think any of us realized how much we would share together over the next year.

On the home front Alanah and I were preparing to move. Our one-year lease in the Bahamas was coming to an end and we did not want to renew. The novelty of living on Paradise Island wore off about a month in. Before the lease was up we looked around different cities in Florida. Living in the Bahamas, I constantly had to connect through Miami, which is quite possibly the worst airport in North America, so Miami was out. A good airport is very high on a wrestler's priority list. After weighing the choices I opted for Tampa. The taxes and cost of living were far cheaper than Canada, they have a great hockey team, the weather is good, and it has a great airport. What more could I ask for? It also seemed that all my Canadian brethren were moving south as well. Andrew, Jay, and Jericho were in the midst of or had already moved there.

In my home office, just chillin'.

Moving to Tampa made going to work much easier. It also didn't hurt that Jay and I were having the time of our lives with the tag team titles. We worked DX, X-Pac, and Road Dogg at *Backlash* in Washington. That night the crowd was on our side, especially after Jay (Christian) split X-Pac open for six stitches with the timekeeper's bell. But little by little the audience was starting to despise our emerging cocky, valley boy, *Bill & Ted's Excellent Adventure*–like personas. Through brainstorming sessions with WWE writer Brian Gerwitz, E&C was truly born. The three of us would just sit and throw around ideas. We created our own vocabulary. Reeking of awesomeness, suckitude, heinosity, and chumpstain all became part of the wrestling fans' vernacular. We would come out to do guest commentary and ad lib.

Reeking of awesomeness, suckitude, heinosity, and chumpstain all became part of the wrestling fans' vernacular.

If you heard us laughing at each other it was legitimate, because we never knew what the other was going to say. The audience could tell we were having a good time pissing them off, and they were biting into our characters like a ripe ol' Granny Smith apple.

We quickly became the heel team that everyone was chasing. We went into a program with Scott Taylor and Brian Christopher, or Scotty 2 Hotty & Grandmaster Sexay. Together they had been calling themselves Too Cool and were doing a white hip-hop gimmick. They were very popular, and it was a natural fit. Scotty and Brian were funny in the ring, but also good workers, and we were the perfect comic foil for their team. We dropped the tag team titles to them in Vancouver with the help of Kid Rock's little rappin' buddy, the late Joe C. Earlier in the night we did a pretape where we "mistook" him for Mini-Me of *Austin Powers* fame. His response was "F$#% you!" Pure Joe C., God rest his soul. At the end of our match, Joe C. exacted his revenge when he ran down and slashed Jay in the berries with a hockey stick. Our first tag team title reign was over and Too Cool were the new champs.

We had a fun series of matches with Too Cool, which got even better with the introduction of Rikishi and Kurt Angle into the mix. Team ECK was born. You may be asking what the hell does that mean, so let me explain. You see, the three of us are very good friends outside of the ring, and the brutal name was an inside joke for our traveling trio that took on a life of its own. Before I go any further, I have to retell an amusing (to everyone except Kurt) Team ECK story from the road. The three of us were riding together, staying in Nashville with a show the next night in Memphis. So after the Nashville show, we grabbed a bite to eat and went to the hotel. My room was next to Kurt's and Jay was down the hall. I hunkered down and had a good night's sleep until about eight A.M., when my phone rang. It was Kurt sounding panicked and saying, "Edge, I need the car keys." (Yes, even in times of distress Kurt still calls me "Edge," not

What do you say to a naked Olympic gold medalist with panic in his eyes?

"Adam.") I threw on some clothes and knocked on his door. When he opened the door, he was butt naked. Now suffice it to say, this had me perplexed. What do you say to a naked Olympic gold medalist with panic in his eyes? If you have an answer, dear reader, let me know. Finally, I noticed that there was blood all over the room and a nasty gash on Kurt's arm. I managed to ask what happened and Kurt proceeded to tell me that his cell phone rang and he jumped up out of a dead sleep to get it. The problem was that his legs were still asleep and he fell face-first into a dresser! He was able to get an arm up but punctured it on the handle. From there, he crawled to answer his phone, leaving a trail of blood all over the room. After all of that, he still didn't get to the phone in time. Talk about adding insult to injury! Now, I have to be honest, it sounds cruel, but I was trying not to laugh. I realized he was going to be fine, and I could not get the mental picture of naked, ghetto-bootied Kurt stumbling around his room trying to get his legs working and taking a faceplant into a dresser! I mean, c'mon, that is kind of comical. I had Kurt put on some clothes and helped him clean up the blood. I offered to take him to the hospital, but, Kurt being Kurt, he said no. He got some stitches and wrestled the Godfather that night in Memphis. For some reason, this story always jumps into my mind when I think of Kurt. Sure, I think of some of the great matches we would have in the future and some of the fun pretapes, but I still can't get the vision of that naked bottom lip hanging and fumbling, stumbling Kurt out of my head.

In the meantime, Jay, Brian, and I had come up with the idea for

a five-second pose before all of our matches. The theory being that we would give our adoring fans a five-second opportunity to snap a picture of their heroes à la a red carpet premiere. At the *No Way Out* PPV in Louisville, Kurt got in on the fun. We were scheduled to face Rikishi and Too Cool in the opening match. Before that could happen, we decided to do the first ever Team ECK five-second pose. After my now mandatory, "For the benefit of those with flash photography, we will now pose for five seconds only! We present to you, the jug band!" We pulled out straw hats, banjos, jugs, horrible buck-toothed dentures, and commenced to pickin' and grinnin'. We looked like ridiculous hay-seeds, and while the Louisville fans knew we were poking fun at them, they still couldn't help but laugh. They did still hate us, though, and we were loving it!

We ended up doing the now infamous five-second pose every week. Some were bound to be duds (funny, my selective memory can't seem to recall any of those). We also had some funny ones. One such pose took place in Detroit right after the mighty Red Wings had been eliminated from the playoffs by the Colorado Avalanche. Jay came out adorned in a goalie mask and a Red Wings jersey. No matter how many times we did it the crowd would initially cheer when we came out with that hometown jersey. And every week we would jerk the carpet out from underneath them. I took off my trench coat to unveil an Avalanche jersey and the boos started to cascade down. Kurt played the role of the referee while I shot an imaginary puck through Jay's legs, and freeze . . . one, two, three, four, five . . . the Hockeytown pose was a great hit! I wrestled Rikishi that night, and as he was about to sit on my face with an extremely large, thong-covered dimpled ass for a move called the Stinkface, Jay put the goalie mask on me. A stroke of genius in the nick of time. We'd found a repellent to the Stinkface!

> Rikishi . . . was about to sit on my face with an extremely large, thong-covered dimpled ass for a move called the Stinkface . . . Jay put the goalie mask on me. A stroke of genius in the nick of time.

Eventually our feud with Too Cool led to the *King of the Ring* and a Four-Way Elimination match in Boston. It was the champs, Too Cool vs. E&C vs. the Hardy Boyz vs. T&A. Of course, with the show being in Boston, you know we had something up our sleeves. That city has just too many bad sports memories to work with, bless its heart. Jay wore a Red Sox jersey to the ring. Once again the crowd bought it and Boston loved E&C. Until I unveiled my New York Mets jersey. Of course we reenacted the infamous Mookie Wilson hit and Bill Buckner bobble that eventually cost them the World Series (oh what we could do with the Chicago Cubs now). Talk about rubbing salt in a gaping wound. It didn't help matters any when Jay clocked Grandmaster with a belt and rolled me on top for the pin and our second tag team championships. Jay and I were definitely riding a wave of unpopularity, but damn it was fun!

With the show being in Boston, you know we had something up our sleeves.

E&C became like herpes. We just kept coming back. It seemed like we were always cheating to hold on to our coveted gold. Because of this it was decided to do the first ever TLC match at *SummerSlam 2000*. All we needed to do was lay the groundwork.

One week while taping *SmackDown!* from the Continental Airlines Arena in New Jersey, we did a five-second pose highlighting my "Oscar win" for my blink-and-you-miss-it appearance in the *Highlander* movie. We froze the pose with Jay (Christian) handing me my prize while I wept like a newborn baby or Tammy Faye

> E&C became like herpes. We just kept coming back.

Bakker at a church revival. After this the Hardys and Dudleyz attacked us. The Duds put Jay through a table while the Hards dropped their Event Omega on me from dual ladders.

The following Monday on *Raw*, Jay and I whined and complained about the unfair treatment we'd been receiving from the Hardys and the Dudleyz, so we were going to stage a sit-down strike right in the middle of the ring. Afterward, Jay got that deer-caught-in-the-headlights look on his face and legitimately forgot what he was going to say. Luckily, Commissioner Mick Foley came out to foil the spoiled brats. This was the beginning of some serious fun that we would have with the Mickster over the coming years, which we have affectionately referred to as Chredgeley (yes, about as bad as Team ECK). The three of us did pretapes where the central theme was sodas ruling the world, surfing lessons at ten P.M., and Jay trying to make weight for the cruiser weight title by wearing a giant chicken suit just so he could have "double gold." It was definitely some of the most fun I've had in the business yet. But on this night, Mick was out to make life a living hell for us. He told us we would be competing in the first ever

TLC match. Tables, ladders, and chairs—oh my! Now it was set. TLC I from the Hardys' backyard in Raleigh, North Carolina.

This time we put pressure on ourselves to live up to our own Triangle Ladder match from *WrestleMania*. Once again we got the "spectacular but safe" speech, this time from Shane McMahon. Good advice, except it was coming from a crazy bastard who had just free-fallen fifty feet in a Hardcore match with Steve Blackman. Of course, being idiots, we had to top that.

The year before, at *SummerSlam,* we went through four teams, including the Hardys, in a Gauntlet match before the Acolytes took our exhausted asses out. But in Raleigh a year later, we were the team to beat. The Dudleyz were the table specialists. The Hardys were the masters of the ladder. We became known as "the chairmen of the WWE" with our illegal finishing move, the Conchairto. Essentially a chair sandwich around our opponents' heads. This war was not going to be pretty.

This war was not going to be pretty.

The crowd in Raleigh was pumped, and so were we, fully expecting to drop the titles to the Hardys in their hometown. Somewhere along the line there was a change in plans. Jay and I had some good heat, so Vince decided to prolong the feud to the next PPV, *Unforgiven* in Philadelphia. At the time, and also in hindsight, I feel the Hardys should have won the title. The prevailing thought was that it would be too predictable, but sometimes predictable is a good thing and it would have been one hell of a moment. I know Matt and Jeff were disappointed, just like we were at *No Mercy*. It didn't stop them from helping put together a memorable and, hell I'll say it, legendary match. Our goal was to steal the show, and we did it again. Although to be fair we had quite a few more props at our disposal.

We had eighteen minutes in which to create, as close as we could, a car wreck in the ring. Chair shots, 3D's through tables, Bubba bombs, hip tosses, powerbombs, and swantons all done from the ladders. We built to a point where everyone was down but the old resilient cockroaches, E&C. We had just pushed Bubba through four tables stacked at ringside in one of the most hellacious and risky bumps ever. As we climbed the whole arena assumed we were about to pull off another one. That is until Lita ran down to the ring. Lita (or Crazy

Leets as I like to call her) had been accompanying, and exciting, crowds with the Hardys for quite a while, but now she was the first, and only, female to join the TLC Club. It added an extra element of excitement, and a great false finish. Plus, she's an awesome person. (Anyone who loves dogs as much as I do is okay in my book.) Lita ran down and shoved Jay and me off the ladder we were climbing for a simultaneous crotch shot on the top rope. This of course left her boyfriend—and hometown hero—Matt, to make the slow climb to the top for the titles. That attempt was foiled by D-Von, who pushed Matt backward through two tables at ringside. I would have been scared to death, but Matt showed his Mattitude and pulled it off. As Lita checked on Matt we came to a point in the match I wasn't all that comfortable with. I was going to spear Crazy Leets. She assured me beforehand that she'd be okay, and to bring it. I knew she'd be hot if I didn't, so I brought it. I brought it so much that her head smashed into a ladder lying at ringside as J.R. screamed, "That son of a bitch!"

How to get real heel heat? Spear Lita.

I saw her head hit and asked her, "You all right, girl?" Luckily she's tough, and other than a goose egg, she assured me she was okay.

Now it was time to bring it home. Matt was down. Bubba was down. Lita was down. D-Von and Jeff were climbing a twelve-foot ladder for the title belts. As they grabbed the belts, Jay and I pulled the ladder from underneath them, and all the air out of the lungs of the fans in attendance. This left them dangling fifteen feet above the ring. It was an awesome sight but I had trouble holding in my laughter. You see, D-Von is deathly afraid of heights. Unfortunately for him he got pigeon-holed into these matches he wanted no part of. So you can imagine how he felt dangling by a cable with Jeff playing foot percussion on his chest. All I could hear was D-Von's terrified voice, "Oh no, not yet, stop kicking, Jeff, oh my God!" I have to hand it to him, he sucked it up and took the nastiest bump this side of Mick Foley in the Hell in a Cell. While I looked at D-Von in shock, Jay grabbed the other ladder lying in the ring. He was supposed to throw it at Jeff and knock him down like a piñata. It proved too awkward, so I ran over and we hurled that ladder like a heavy javelin into Jeff's rib cage. He landed and we set the eight-foot ladder under the now wildly swinging title belts. Too short. So we grabbed the monster ladder and climbed to our belts for a successful title defense and a seriously pissed off crowd.

We got to the back and once again the boys made it all the more special. Kudos from your peers feel almost as good as the crowd reaction. Almost. The next night on *Raw,* while we licked our wounds, the feud with the Hardys raged on.

E&C's five-second poses allowed me to expand my hockey jersey collection.

CHAPTER

The E&C Dynasty (as we now humbly titled ourselves) had made a promise in the likely event we won the TLC match. We promised the first, and last ever, thirty-seven-second pose! Why, you ask, thirty-seven? Why not? The monumental pose would take place on *Raw*. As we prepared to hit our world record pose we were interrupted by the Dudleyz music. But to our utter surprise (wink, wink) it wasn't the Dudleyz but two midgets who bore a striking resemblance to Bubba and D-Von. They made their way to the ring with a furious gleam in their eye and a deadly plastic table in hand! We asked the mini-Dudleyz what their problem was. Mini Bubba responded with a hearty "Whassuuuuuppp!" While Mini D-Von (who had worked on his performance all day) barely responded "Testify!" Right about this time in our story the Hardys music filled the arena, but once again a somewhat smaller version of the Hardys came out. They made

> They made their way to the ring with a furious gleam in their eye and a deadly plastic table in hand!

their way to the ring with horrible wigs atop their skulls and a plastic toy ladder. As Mini Matt bellowed uncontrollably, Mini Jeff didn't make a peep.

This of course led to our Earth-shattering, jaw-dropping, mind-blowing, record-breaking thirty-seven-second pose. As we held the titles high above the smaller versions of the Duds and the Hards, they ran around us in circles leaping in vain for the gold. As cruel and "un-PC" as it sounds, to this day I still laugh when I picture it. About twenty seconds into our pose the real Hardys stormed the ring and lambasted us with the plastic furniture. It was a fun segment that paved the way for our next two promos. The first involved an older version of Matt, Jeff, and

Lita. We claimed we had an E&C Time Machine and we brought back Team Extreme from the year 2056. Not quite as memorable as the midgets. Actually, it was only memorable for the fact that our elderly Team Extreme forgot all of their lines, and geriatric Lita looked quite disturbing in a half shirt and exposed thong.

Geriatric Lita looked quite disturbing in a half shirt and exposed thong.

The next installment of E&C's comedy hour took place backstage in Chicago. I love Chicago. It's a unanimous vote throughout the locker room that Chi-Town is our best crowd. It's also the home of movie critics Roger Ebert and the late Gene Siskel. Jay (Christian), Brian, and I all thought we should become movie critics for the night. Chriskel and Edgebert were born! We would be critiquing home movies. More specifically, the early home movies of Matthew and Jeffrey Hardy, where they were trying to iron out their wrestling characters with some b-r-utal prematch promos. To be fair to my buddies, they were very young, and let's face it, any serious wrestling fan did the same thing. Although that didn't mean Jay and I wouldn't exploit it. The Hardys are great sports and were totally cool with the idea. That was the great part about our angle. No backstage politics, just good business and fun.

While Team Extreme were in the ring after a match, Chriskel and Edgebert splashed up on the Titantron. We commenced to tear the Hardys teenage exploits to shreds. Bless their hearts, it was like beating baby seals. They stormed from the ring into the dressing room area only to be "Pearl Harbored" by the chairmen of WWE. We hit Matt from behind, who crashed into Lita and rammed her into a wall. We decked Jeff with a chair while screaming that they didn't have what it takes. This was our go-home show leading into *Unforgiven* and a tag team title match to take place within the confines of a fifteen-foot steel cage.

While a hometown win for the Hardys in TLC would have been nice, the Cage match in Philly lived up to the rest of the feud. Both members of the team had to hit the floor or obtain one pinfall. Early in the match (in hindsight maybe too early) Jeff went to the top of the cage for one of his insane dives. Before he could dive I pushed him from the cage to the floor, which essentially eliminated him from the match. This left Matt all alone to be bloodied by us. Originally none of us were supposed to get color during the match. The culmination of our feud was a Cage match in Philadelphia, the birthplace of ECW, and no blood! The Philly fans would be mortified. We went to Vince and he agreed, but only one of us could do it. Due to the setup of the match Matt volunteered. So now Matt was down and out. I had the keys to the cage down my tights (which I stole from Jeff earlier). E&C were well on their way to another victory until Jay climbed out to stop Jeff from coming in. It backfired when Jeff knocked him off the cage with a ladder. Jeff then used the ladder to climb to the top of the cage. As he did you could see the whole crowd rise to their feet in anticipation. As Matt and I pulled ourselves off the mat from my top rope bulldog (during which I almost dropped a hot bag of mud in my tights), Jeff jumped. I swear he floated. He executed his corkscrew "whisper in the wind," knocking all of us down.

In the meantime Jay had climbed the ladder on the outside trying to get back in. As he did, Lita (who was "injured" in Chicago) came down, climbed the cage, and did a hurracanrana from the cage, off the ladder, to the floor. It was a risky move, but she pulled it off like a champ. She was such an important fixture in this angle. Before the crowd could cool down, I made the slow, amputeelike crawl up the cage. Matt and Jeff followed with the two chairs Jay and I had brought in beforehand. I have to admit, I was not looking forward to this next portion of the match. As I reached the top the Hardys stopped me and lined me up for their version of a Conchairto from the top of the cage. I was comfortable with the chair shot. I've been hit so many times with steel chairs that the top of my head now officially smells like ass. I was a little nervous about the bump afterward, though. But Matt assured me it would be okay, as I would be unconscious on the way down. He was joking, but his words were all too prophetic.

I hit the mat like a rag doll, or a crash-test dummy.

After the Conchairto, all I heard was ringing. I hit the mat like a rag doll, or a crash-test dummy. Matt and Jeff hit the floor as the new Tag Team Champions. It was a great moment for all of us, but especially the Hardys. I think they were wondering if they'd ever get those titles back. As they celebrated, I tried to sit up. It just wasn't working. Timmy White slowly helped me from the cage while the arena spun and I tried not to puke. I received five stitches, without freezing, because, as the doctor said, "Wrestlers are tough." After that experience I say bullshit, give me the freezing. I stumbled back to my hotel with a concussion and the notion that we would probably have *Raw,* the next night, off.

Once again I would be wrong. Very wrong. Jay and I got to the building to find out we were doing a Ladder match with the Hardys. Fittingly it was at Penn State, the sight of our emotional promo the night after the original Ladder match. That still didn't mean we were ready to do it. We were all beat to hell, but it was the first *Raw* on TNN, and the writers wanted to load the show with as many big matches as possible. In that respect it was a compliment, but it was still gonna hurt! After finding out we had a Ladder match, we also found out we had only seven minutes in which to do it. Let me put that into perspective for you, dear Edgehead. At *No Mercy* we had twenty minutes. At *WrestleMania* we had twenty-eight minutes. TLC I had eighteen minutes. All healthy amounts of time to put together a Ladder match and sell everything properly. At seven minutes a good Ladder match is next to impossible. We were told it didn't have to live up to our other Ladder matches, but to us it did.

We ended up getting thirteen minutes, which quickly turned to eighteen halfway through the match. Even with the added time it still didn't quite live up to the others. It did mark the first time I used my "super spear" from the ladder with Jeff hanging from the belts, but it still ranks as my least favorite. According to a Commissioner Foley edict before the match, this would be our first and last shot for the titles while the Hardys had them. We lost, and that would bring about the return of one of WWE's most infamous and legendary teams: Los Conquistadors!!

Los Conquistadors. I'm the good-looking one on the right.

To find a loophole in Mick's decree we resurrected Los Conquistadors. I was Unos and Jay was Dos. In between Speedy Gonzalez sound effects all we said was "Si, señor" and "Papi Chulo" (a Mexican wrestler with the company at the time). The original Conquistadors were a lower-card team during the eighties. They wore horrible gold bodysuits with matching gold masks. Our seamstresses, Julie and Terri, scrambled to make some shiny new gold outfits for us. It was not the most flattering look, made only worse by the masks we had to wear. They didn't have time to make them so some Mexican wrestling masks were purchased at the local head shop and spray-painted gold. Every time I wrestled as Unos I got a contact high from the fumes.

Every time I wrestled as Unos I got a contact high from the fumes.

Everyone knew it was us, but we still disguised ourselves with a ridiculous trot down to the ring followed by simultaneous rolls. We were luchadores, hola! The Conquistadors were entered in a tag team battle royal to determine the number one contenders for the titles. Wrestling as fearlessly (and clumsily) as only the Conquistadors could, we won the battle royal for a shot at the Hardys and their titles in Albany at *No Mercy*.

Heading to the PPV we did some humorous business as always with Mick Foley. We had two impostor Conquistadors (played by indy wrestlers Christopher Daniels and Aaron Aguilera) who would show up beside us as we declared them our "totally favorite tag team!"

No Mercy was rolling around and E&C, as the Conquistadors, were winning the title for the third time. I had to wear two spray-painted masks for the match. It was brutal, and the match wasn't all that much better. I still don't know how anyone can wrestle under a mask. During the match Jay went for his "jimmy jump" over the ropes to the floor. Let's take a little time-out here. Before we get to the outcome of the move, I thought you may be asking yourself what the hell is a jimmy jump? Let me explain. We coined the term because of Matt Hardy's very odd legs. His hip sockets are all messed up, which causes what we call "the jimmy legs." The poor guy can't even do a squat, his knees shoot out in every direction. After that, everything became jimmy this, jimmy that, leading to the coup de grâce of you're jimmied. Well, Jay got jimmied on his jimmy jump. He'd never done it with a mask on and as he did it shifted over his eyes. He was in midair, fifteen feet above the floor, falling blindly. After he careened off Matt he took

It happened so quickly none of us realized he was hurt.

a nosedive into the floor. He landed awkwardly and lost the feeling in his right arm (he's had problems ever since). It happened so quickly none of us realized he was hurt. The finish came as Matt pulled off my mask to reveal . . . another mask, at which point Jay hit his Unprettier, jimmy arm hanging limply by his side, to gain the pin and E&C's third tag title reign.

This reign was short-lived. The next night on *Raw* we maneuvered ourselves into a title shot against Los Conquistadors. We would have our replacements in the ring and beat them for the title. All was working in our devious plan until the Dudleyz put Jay through a table backstage because he couldn't work with his injured neck and shoulder. Knowing the fix was in I bravely volunteered to take on both Conquistadors myself and bring the title home. As I waited in the ring, Unos and Dos made their way down, both sporting a full-on jimmy walk. That's right, the Hardys beat up our replacements and replaced them. I fought valiantly (yes, that's sarcasm) but I succumbed to a twist of fate, swanton combination for the loss. As I wondered what the hell happened the Conquistadors took off their masks to reveal the Hardys. It actually got a nice surprising reaction from the crowd, considering they had just seen them hit signature Hardy moves. It was a confusing story line at times, but I think it all made sense in the end.

After this program E&C would float for a couple of months. The Hardys dropped the title to the RTC, The Goodfather and Bull Buchanan. *Survivor Series* was in Tampa, Florida, and we teamed with RTC against the Hards and Duds.

Finally, at the December PPV, *Armageddon* from Birmingham, Alabama, we were in an elimination four-way along with the Duds, RTC, and K-Kwik & Road Dogg. We assumed the Dudleyz would go over but were surprised when Michael Hayes told us we were taking the title for the fourth time. I don't remember the match being all that memorable, besides pinning the Duds for the final fall leading to a match with them at *Royal Rumble*. But before we could get to the *Rumble*, we had to go through Undertaker and The Rock. *Uh-oh!* I had a great time working with these guys. We were in the main events and the audience accepted us there. We belonged! We also had two back-to-back matches with them that were damn good, if I do say so myself! On *Raw*, the night after *Armageddon*, we dropped the title to them. The next night, on *SmackDown!*, we beat them with a Conchairto on Rock to tie the record for tag team title reigns with our fifth win. Like I said, I loved working with those guys, but they had their own angle and we had the Dudleyz to contend with.

Now that I have compared Jay and myself to herpes and cockroaches, let me set the stage for another E&C title match during February's *No Way Out* in Las Vegas. It was E&C vs. Dudleyz vs. Undertaker & Kane, all three of which are "brother teams." It did not end up being a very good night for me. About five minutes into the title match my back locked up. I was unable to even lift my feet. I had to shimmy across the ring like the old man I was quickly becoming and tell 'Taker, "My back is messed up!" He responded with, "How bad?"

This was pretty bad. I thought, "I can't lift my feet!" From that point on I did what I could. It was then relayed to everyone that I was hurt, but we still had about twelve minutes to go. By the end of the match I tried, very unsuccessfully, to spear myself through a table. I had all the speed of a roaring tortoise and

> As I cooled down and the adrenaline wore off, the pain got worse.

bounced off the table to an audible groan from the crowd. Bubba grabbed me and said, "Would you please just lay down?" as he tossed me from the ring. However, my night was not done. I still had 'Taker's chokeslam to survive. As I slowly pulled myself into the ring he hooked me in the goozle and said, "Don't worry, kid, nice and easy, I got you!" And he did. It looked great and didn't hurt too bad, although at that point I think I was numb.

As I cooled down and the adrenaline wore off, the pain got worse. We had a Southwest Airlines flight after the show to Phoenix, Arizona. They actually put me in a wheelchair to get me on and off the airplane. Finally, at about three A.M., we arrived in Phoenix, where I shared a room with my good buddy Rhyno, who at the time was doing dark matches with WWE. As unmanly as it sounds, he had to take my pants off for me and help me lay down. It was pretty pathetic. The next day

I got to the building and was told to go home. The office had already made an appointment for me to get an MRI done back in Tampa.

The MRI revealed I had two protruding discs in my lower back. It also revealed a hairline fracture in the front of my skull, which had healed nicely. Especially considering I never knew anything about it prior to this MRI, but it explained a lot for my lack of mental faculties! It took me three weeks of rest and rehab before I was able to go back to work, and I was back in time for Rhyno's WWE debut and yet another E&C title win.

The Hardys had somehow managed to get the titles again and the Dudleyz were set to challenge them on an episode of *Raw* from Albany, New York. According to the story line, someone (I wonder who!) had changed the Dudleyz flight. Conveniently we just "happened" to be there to take their spot. When it looked as though Jeff had the match won, Rhyno made his debut goring Jeff out of his boots, as Paul Heyman screamed "Gore! Gore! Gore!" on commentary. One pinfall later, Jay and I owned the record for the most tag team title reigns ever out of any other tag teams in WWE history! Never in my wildest dreams did I ever think we would accomplish that when we were jumping off his parents' washing machine back in Orangeville.

Once again our title reign was short-lived. The Dudleyz arrived during the show and challenged us, obviously, instead of the Hardys for the Tag Team title. This was the match where Spike Dudley debuted, hitting his Dudley Dawg to help them win their third tag title. Now you had a trifecta of three-member units. The Hardys with Lita. The Dudleyz with Spike, and us with Rhyno. It was a good dichotomy, leading us all to *WrestleMania X-Seven* in Houston, Texas. In the weeks leading up to this *WrestleMania,* Rhyno eliminated both Spike and Lita from the equation. The last *SmackDown!* show before the PPV saw the Dudleyz and the Hardys eliminate Rhyno, leaving the stage set for us to shine! *WrestleMania X-Seven!* TLC II in front of almost seventy thousand people at the Houston Astrodome. This would be the biggest crowd any of us had wrestled in front of, which I think may have added a little tension to the mix. We found out the night before that, once again, the reigning kings of nonsuckitude were going over, adding even more tension.

Later, all three tag teams sat down with Michael Hayes to put the match together. The tension came to a head when we came to the finish of the match. Basically, it boiled down to a bunch of guys with a passion for the business who really cared about how the match would end. Strangely, Matt and I were the ones disagreeing. Unlike Jeff Hardy's version, which he wrote in their book, it would never have come to blows. It was a heated debate between two perfectionists. So, to all of you M-Fers reading this, don't roast me on a spit because we worked it out and he is still one of my closest friends.

After we hashed everything out, my finish was outvoted. It is a good thing, too, because I think it worked better after everything was all said and done. It's strange, but I don't get nervous before my matches, big or small. I don't really know why either. I do get amped up, but not nervous. On that night, when Jay and I went out to the ring, I stopped, just for an extra two seconds, to soak in the size and electricity of that crowd of seventy thousand. It was insane!

I stopped, just for an extra two seconds, to soak in the size and electricity of that crowd of seventy thousand. It was insane!

This match had a lot of ingredients that helped make it a tasty morsel for anyone watching. I would like to think the fans got their money's worth in that match alone, not to forget all of the other amazing matches that took place that night. During our match it was a little tough for me to gauge the crowd's reaction. In a dome that size the sound travels straight up and not directly at you, like it does in smaller arenas. Don't get me wrong, I would take this over six people in a barn any day. Watching a tape of the match after the show, we were all much happier with the results than we were right after it was over. We had a run-in by Spike. He gave me a Dudley Dawg and gave Jay a Dudley Dawg over the top and to the floor and through a table to chants of ECW. Now it was Rhyno's turn. He ripped through the ring like a tornado in a trailer park and gored Matt through a table in the corner. He set up a ladder for me and I started to climb. Before I could get to the top, Lita ran down and jerked me off . . . the ladder! (that was J.R.'s unintentionally funny commentary). Now Lita, Spike, and Rhyno had a cool exchange. Rhyno pressed Lita over his head. Spike hit Rhyno in the "berries" while Lita went to the top rope to hit her Litacarana, allowing Spike to blast Rhyno with a chair into one of the ladders. It just so happened I was climbing that ladder, and as I got the tip of my finger on one of the belts, Rhyno knocked the ladder over, sending me into my favorite Ladder match bump, the top rope crotch killer!

Lita grabbed a chair and initiated Spike into the TLC Club with a very wicked chair shot. Contrary to popular belief, the chairs, tables, and ladders are all very real. Home Depot's finest! Lita peeled off her shirt, turned, and got 3D'ed for lookin' sexy. Next Rhyno was on the receiving end of the Dudleyville Device. Jeff set up the fifteen-foot ladder on the floor and placed Rhyno and Spike on two tables side by side. One huge swanton later and Spike Dudley was missing his front teeth. As far as I know, that was the worst casualty of the match, along with the seventeen staples Matt had to get in his head. Now, Jay and D-Von were on top of the same lad-

der, grabbing at the belts when Matt pulled the ladder out, leaving D-Von hanging above the ring once again! Only this time he was hanging there with Jay instead of Jeff and begging him to stop kicking! D-Von was scared to death, but finally both he and Jay bumped to the mat far below. Jeff had come up with the great idea of walking across

One huge swanton later and Spike Dudley was missing his front teeth . . . that was the worst casualty of the match, along with the seventeen staples Matt had to get in his head.

the top of three of the ladders to get the belts, which he almost pulled off, but the third ladder tipped, sending him down. I almost liked that better. It really raised the crowd's anticipation. Jeff eventually made it to the belts and grabbed them, only this time Bubba had grabbed the ladder and walked it to the opposite corner with Jeff's feet still hooked to it. All the while I was climbing the monster ladder in the opposite corner readying myself for Jeff to swing my way. Jeff came at me so I leaped off. The timing was perfect. I hit the superspear from way above in the "Showcase of the Immortals." The crowd visibly bounced with the move and to this day it is still the move I get asked about the most. I was seeing stars from doing that move, so I can't imagine how Jeff must have felt, although I think he is quite possibly the best bumper in the business.

Everyone was down except Matt and Bubba, who climbed the monster ladder only to have Rhyno tip it, causing them to crash through four tables piled at ringside. You could see the crowd rise to their feet as Matt and Bubba fell. It looked deadly. And it was a little odd to hear seventy thousand people scream "Holy shit!" By this point Rhyno grabbed Jay, put him on his shoulders, and climbed the ladder while I held D-Von. Jay grabbed the belts, making our record that much harder to catch. It would make us seven-time Tag Team Champions and the winners of the Triangle Ladder match, TLC I and TLC II (not that I'm rubbing it in, guys!).

It was a little odd to hear seventy thousand people scream "Holy shit!"

It was a relief to get that one over and done with, relatively unscathed. That would be the last time Jay and I would win the titles (for now). We eventually lost them to Kane and Undertaker. Hey, my take on it is, if you're gonna lose the title, you may as well lose them to the biggest and the baddest!

E&C, one last time before the split...

Coming off the best run of our careers, Jay and I were hit with a situation we never thought we'd find ourselves in. It was much more serious than a story line or a TLC match. One Monday, while out in the arena ironing out what we would do on that night's telecast of *Raw* from MSG, J.R. approached saying he needed to talk to us and that we should sit down. Anytime someone says that it's invariably bad news. I rolled through my mental Rolodex of what the problem could be. Money, contract, attitude problem? I couldn't come up with anything, but what J.R. said was the absolute last thing I had in mind. He said that a woman from Nashville, Tennessee, was accusing Jay and me of raping her. I cannot effectively explain the feeling of my stomach falling and the complete and utter silence that MSG now seemed to hold. My world had been flipped upside down. I went through a myriad of emotions—shock, disbelief, sadness, and finally anger. I was pissed off because I knew this was bullshit. We offered to take whatever tests we needed to then and there. J.R. said he and Vince knew it couldn't be true but we didn't want the media to get wind of it. No matter our innocence, people would still come to their own conclusions, fair or not. Jay was recently married and I was well on my way. I couldn't get my head around why someone would do this. Apparently the woman couldn't remember the day of this alleged incident. So while she tried to decide what day she was supposedly raped by two WWE wrestlers, my stomach was tied in knots. I told Alanah and she was totally supportive. After a week, our accuser "picked" a day. The day she picked we were performing in front of ten thousand eyewitnesses in Spokane, Washington. We were nowhere near Tennessee during that time frame. To this day I still can't fathom

> I went through a myriad of emotions— shock, disbelief, sadness, and finally anger.

177

why someone would try to ruin another person's life. Hopefully I never will learn why.

Now that we had that fiasco behind us, we moved into a tag feud with the two Chrises: Benoit and Jericho. It is not remembered all that well, but it is still one of my favorite series of matches. Four Canadians beating the stuffing out of one another. You would have thought that it was a Saturday night in a Moosejaw, Saskatchewan, bar the way we all went at it. The series led to the grand finale, which became known as the forgotten TLC match (at least by the participants). The night before, Triple H tore his quad and Austin was taking a break. Because of this, everyone thought we needed a TLC match. TLC III on *Smack-Down!* in Anaheim, California, for Benoit and Jericho's newly won tag team titles. TLC III was to be the Dudleyz, the Hardys, E&C, and now Benoit & Jericho. That day I voiced my concern that TLC matches are, and should be, PPV matches. I still stand by that opinion and probably always will. I just don't think you should put Hell in a Cell on TV for free

The "forgotten" TLC match, Jericho and I.

nor a TLC match. They are dangerous matches and that is what makes them special. You desensitize how punishing TLC matches can truly be. Hindsight is always 20/20.

You desensitize how punishing TLC matches can truly be. Hindsight is always 20/20.

Sometimes extenuating circumstances force your hand, so we all shrugged and went out there and tore it up. The Pond in Anaheim has definitely witnessed some classic TLC action. I believe this is the match where Benoit first injured his neck, which later needed fusion. After this it felt as though Jay and I were close to wearing out our welcome as a team. It was time to cut the cord and go our separate ways. We had feuded with every team, leaving us really no where else to go. My goal in this business is to be the world champ, and you can't do that in a tag team. We had started planting the seeds for our split leading up to the *King of the Ring 2001* tournament. The final four boiled down to Rhyno, Kurt Angle, Jay, and myself—on TV and off, four friends. I went over Rhyno in the semis while Kurt topped Jay. I think everyone assumed it would be Jay and me in the finals. Brother vs. Brother and then the obvious split happens. It probably would have been a good place to do it, but instead, Kurt and I began what was to be the first chapter in a very long feud over the next few years. It was the first time Kurt and I worked each other in front of a PPV audience. Disappointingly, it was only okay. I was off and Kurt was concussed from his match with Jay. Our agent Jack Lanza prepared for the fact that we may take it home very early, that is how incoherent Kurt was. I talked him through it (a favor he would return to me later in a Fatal Fourway match in Dallas). We stumbled through it and the end result was still one of my career highlights. After a Shane McMahon run-in and an Edgeacution (my new DDT move, which I stole from the departed Gangrel), I was the *King of the Ring 2001* champion. The only thing that made it better was the fact that it happened in the home of my beloved New Jersey Devils, the Meadowlands in East Rutherford. In my postmatch interviews I claimed the "Era of Awesomeness" had begun! I would be the second to last *King of the Ring* winner. Brock Lesnar was the 2002 winner and the PPV was changed the following year. Coming off my win, the next night, I was presented with my trophy in a coronation ceremony,

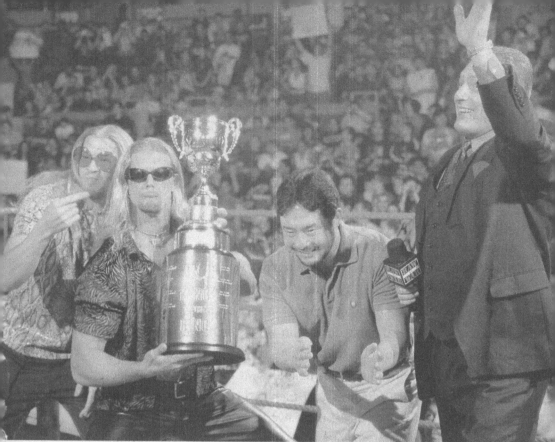

"Graciously" accepting my <u>King of the Ring</u> trophy.

MSG-style. Billy Gunn would interrupt. Bad move, since I then tore him to shreds verbally. I stated that he, Billy Bitchcakes, was like a human vacuum cleaner, managing to both suck and blow at the same time! Yes, I "borrowed" it from *The Simpsons*, but hey, that show is comic genius.

He . . . was like a human vacuum cleaner, managing to both suck and blow at the same time!

After the verbal beating Jay grabbed my trophy and started a two-month love affair with it that in turn helped water the seeds of the split. The classic story line of jealousy was brewing, only to be put on hold to simmer while another pivotal moment in the wrestling industry began.

WWE bought out our main and only competition on television, WCW, thus starting the invasion angle. Because it was company versus company, having two WWE stars feuding may have been left on the back burner, and Jay and I wanted the E&C split to mean something. We continued to team during this time, and to our surprise found the crowd cheering. They had finally given in. We worked Lance Storm and Mike Awesome in the first "official" company versus company match at the *Invasion* PPV. The reason, you ask? Well, being the kings of reeking with awesomeness, how dare anyone else use "awesome" in their ring moniker. That and the fact that Lance despised our "off-beat shenanigans."

After almost walking into the large hole in the middle of the *Invasion* ramp, we went on to have a halfway decent match. At one point Jay attempted a dive to the floor off my back. On paper it seemed like a good idea. We just didn't calculate the sweat factor. He slipped off my back and took a nosedive over the top of the ropes to the floor. Lance and Mike were able to corral him before he broke his neck. After keeping Lance in the match as much as possible we went on to pin Mike and moved on to *SummerSlam.*

Between *Invasion* and *SummerSlam,* Lance won the I-C title. Still being a detractor of our "off-beat shenanigans," it was a gimmie for Edge to take Lance on for the I-C title at *SummerSlam* in San Jose, California. In the meantime Jay and I pitched the idea to Vince to allow us to have our split in Toronto, our hometown. What better place than in front of our "family" and friends? *Raw* from Toronto was two weeks after *SummerSlam,* so our I-C title match became another vehicle in fueling the jealousy between E&C. Lance and I kicked off *SummerSlam* that year and we kicked it off right. I am very proud of that match, it still stands out as one of my personal favorites. Lance is one of my best friends, inside and outside the ring. He is a family man, a class act, and a pure joy to work with.

I had come up with a spot the week before that would have Jay "accidentally" spear me during my and Lance's match. I thought it would be a great false finish and help boost the story of our split. The day of the show I was told by our agent that we could not use a run-in. I felt pretty strongly about this one and so did Lance, so I took it to Vince. After explaining my thought process Vince agreed. In my opinion, it ended up being the best sequence in the match. So, after Jay's botched spear on me we went home with an Edgeacution and I was once again the I-C champion, except this time it was supposed to happen. After the match Jay stood behind me holding the title belt. The crowd was expecting the inevitable turn, but instead he handed

Winning back the I-C title.

me the title belt, hugged me, and it left the crowd wondering when the split would come.

It finally happened on September 3, 2001. It was at the ACC in Toronto, Canada. Jay and I were both emotional. This was a big deal to us. We were ending something special to take a gamble on trying to make it on our own. Jay worked The Rock early in the

We were ending something special to take a gamble on trying to make it on our own.

show for the WCW title. The crowd was behind Jay, which I think legitimately upset The Rock, but hey, Canuckleheads are loyal to their own. Rock won the match and this brought the Creepy Little Bastard to his breaking point. Later in the evening I once again worked Lance and defended the I-C title. After the match was over, Lance attacked my knee, which brought Jay back out. He stormed the ring with a chair to save the day. The chair in his hand was a dead giveaway, but instead of the expected chair shot he hugged me.

Therefore the crowd was shocked when he finally did lace me with that Home Depot special. From there Jay went postal, making Michael Douglas in *Falling Down* look sane. He grabbed my *King of the Ring* trophy and held it high over his head as if he was on the '67 Leafs doing a victory lap with Lord Stanley's Cup, bringing it down to his lips and kissing it (which, I mentally noted to myself, was a nice touch). But nice was not in his game plan when he took the trophy and slammed it down into my ribs. By the way, Jay, because I know you're reading this, that really hurt! Afterward he said he brought it down gently. (Gently, my ass!) He brought it down more like a scud missile. The whole maneuver set me up for his evil finale. A one-man Conchairto. It looked pretty damn vile, especially as he ripped his own hair out, looking pretty damn insane to me! As I lay there looking at Jay I felt a little saddened because

It looked pretty damn vile, especially as he ripped his own hair out, looking pretty damn insane to me!

we were ending an era, although at the same time I felt happy that the angle seemed to go over very well. I was also a little groggy from the beating he laid on me. Later that night I received a message from Benoit, who was complimenting my selling job. (At the time, he was at home recovering from his spinal fusion surgery.) It was great to hear such positive feedback from someone I respect so much. Trust me, though, when Jay swings a chair he thinks he is Sammy Sosa, corked bat and all, leaving me no choice but to sell it. Our program was off to a good start. Too bad the rest of the angle didn't quite live up to our initial split.

Jay and I put a lot of pressure on ourselves to make sure our angle went well. We ended up psyching ourselves out. After the split, I was off the show for two weeks. During that time I worked with our creative producer Kevin Dunn to get permission to use a song from Rob Zombie's upcoming CD, *The Sinister Urge.* I knew it wasn't going to be released until November of that year, but I wanted new music to coincide with this new chapter in my career, so I took a shot in the dark. I had always been a huge fan of Rob's music. As a matter of fact, the first time I heard his music was while I was getting my first tattoo (yes, Hunter, the street shark!) at Artatorture Tattoos in Toronto with Fatty. Luckily the Zombie camp was all ears and I was sent an advanced copy from which I picked the track "Never Gonna Stop." It summed up perfectly the mind-set I wanted the new character to have. Never gonna stop until I get that world title!

With my new music set, it was time to return. I did it with a bang! Actually, quite a few bangs, which were landed squarely on Jay's head and face. Oh yeah, payback time for that chair shot/trophy barrage!

It was the most intense I'd ever felt in a wrestling ring at that point in my career, and it showed. Once again this was a success, and Jay walked away with only a bloody lip. It was all leading up to a match for *Unforgiven,* where I would be fighting to keep my I-C title.

Unforgiven took place in Pittsburgh, Pennsylvania. When we saw that Pittsburgh was the city in which we would fight our first match, we collectively groaned. No offense to the "Steel City," but unless you are Kurt Angle or a large flying projectile named Mick Foley, it is usually hard to get much of anything out of a Pittsburgh crowd. Part of the reason is because we work there at least six times a year; so, like Jersey and New York, they've seen it all (that and the fact that the citizens of Pittsburgh have to claim the Penguins as their hockey team, which doesn't help). Still, if you are good enough you can get the crowd into it. That night only one match was able to bring Pittsburgh to its feet and get the crowd going: Kurt Angle's match. Their native son won the world title and the house came down.

I remember lying in the ring afterward, my eye swollen shut from the thick gash under it, thinking we let ourselves down.

Jay and I couldn't get it done that night. For the finish, I set Jay up so I could perform my own one-man Conchairto and get some retribution, but it was not to be. The referee grabbed the chair from my hands, I turned my back and Jay hit me in the grapefruits with the other chair for his first I-C title. It was an okay match, but it was not our best, not what we were capable of. In a strange way we were trying too hard. I remember lying in the ring afterward, my eye swollen shut from the thick gash under it, thinking we let ourselves down. It was still an intense match—as evidenced by the four stitches we each had to get afterward—but we were disappointed. We would just have to make up for it next time around.

We both really wanted our solo careers to succeed (like I said before), and I think because we wanted it so bad, we began to second-guess ourselves. When we teamed together we never did that, which is why we were so successful. From a personal standpoint I went from being in *the* heel tag team to being a singles babyface—a huge transition, and I think the crowd could feel my lack of confidence. Actually, I didn't get into my singles groove until the brand extension. Like the Hardy's eventual split, I am not sure the audience really wanted to see us fight each other.

Luckily, not long down the road Jay and I got our "next time." Jay had joined the Alliance (WCW/ECW) and commenced to lay me out weekly with his Alliance goons. We had a Ladder match set for *No Mercy* in October. St. Louis would be the place we would once again feud for the title. The feud started to gain back some of its earlier momentum. This Ladder match was to be our blow off. When the angle got some of its mojo back the writers thought we might be able to get to another PPV bout. If the Ladder match hadn't already been set, I might have agreed. The way I saw it was, if I were to get beat in a match with no rules, why would any fan want to see it again for a third time? Where do you go from a Ladder match? Hell in a Cell? We were not high enough on the totem pole. TLC? Impossible for two guys to sell it properly. If a babyface loses a Ladder match that is the end of the angle.

Finally, on the day of the show, it was decided the feud between E&C was over and I would win my third I-C title. When people had seen us in previous Ladder matches, there were always at least four or six other bodies to bump around. Obviously this was not the case here, meaning a lot more down time between bumps. Now it was just us, so we had to slow things down and sell everything properly. We may have slowed it down too much. I definitely gained a new measure of respect for what Shawn Michaels and Razor Ramon did in *WrestleMania X*.

Once again we beat the hell out of each other, especially because the physicality gets turned up a few notches when ladders are involved. Looking back I can laugh, but poor Jay thought he'd crushed

The meaning of <u>No Mercy</u>.

his gonads at one point. If you watch a tape of the match you can see Jay groping his Mannheim (my pet name for the male reproductive area) to see if his little buddies were still intact! Good thing they were, too, because at the end of the match I hit Jay in the grapes again. This time with a chair, which he had done to me the previous

Hey, paybacks are a bitch!

month in our *Unforgiven* match. Hey, paybacks are a bitch! This finish really sticks out in my mind, but not in Jay's, since I knocked him out cold with a one man Conchairto on top of two ladders. I remember thinking to myself, "Man that was a great sell, he looks like a human slinky!" Much to his dismay, he wasn't selling. That was a tough match for him, not to mention that he had to drop the title to me to top it all off, bless his heart!

From there things got hectic. I flew to Albuquerque to introduce Rob Zombie for his Merry Mayhem tour with Ozzy Osbourne. Another great perk of the biz! This was cooler than Samuel L. Jackson in *Pulp Fiction*. I got to the arena and met Rob walking his dog, Dracula (go figure), out back. We hit it off pretty well and got to know quite a bit about each other. He thought I had been forced to use his music and wanted to get the appearance over with as soon as possible. After I buzzed him on my tattoo story and what a big fan I was we hit his dressing room. We sat around drinking tea and Red Bulls with his wife, Sheri, and the rest of the band. Sorry to burst the rock 'n' roll bubble, but it really was tea and Red Bull! Sharon Osbourne made an appearance and asked me if I played guitar, she thought I looked like a clean Zakk Wylde (one of my buds and Ozzy's guitarist). Regrettably I didn't get to meet the ol' Blizzard of Ozz but I still had one hell of a time.

Rob had talked me into wearing my wrestling gear onstage. I still kick myself for that one, but on Rob's psychedelic, monster-themed, hot-rod stage I didn't look out of place. As a matter of fact, I probably looked the most normal. Rob introduced me to the crowd before they played "Never Gonna Stop." I cut a quick promo

I was banging my head like a kid from the eighties caught in a mosh at an Anthrax concert.

and stayed onstage for the rest of the song. I was banging my head like a kid from the eighties caught in a mosh at an Anthrax concert. I also unknowingly ended up doing a duet with Rob. Earlier I had hit my mic to make sure it was turned off. I still thought it was off when I began singing. Those poor souls in Albuquerque were assaulted by my vocal stylings. Take Steve Austin's brutal singing ability, lower it about ten notches, and you have my singing voice. I didn't realize my mic was on until the video aired on

Those poor souls in Albuquerque were assaulted by my vocal stylings.

Raw a week later. Oh well, it was better than Vince singing "Stand Back" on the wrestling album. Now *that* should have been outlawed!

After Rob was done I watched some of Ozzy's show from Zakk's sound board before I had to leave. With my ears still ringing I went back to the hotel and packed for my 5:45 A.M. flight to England for a PPV Cage match against Jay.

I landed in jolly ole England running on only four hours of sleep out of the last forty-eight. My tank was empty. Even so, the Cage match ended up being the best televised match of our program. We had the old classic blue cage (which hurts like hell). We did a cool spot where Jay was about to jump to the floor and win back the I-C title, but before he could, I grabbed his feet and pulled his legs through making him hit the cage—groin first! (Jay's poor nuts seem to be a reoccurring theme in our feud!) From there I took my wrist tape and hog-tied his feet together. While he hung upside down reaching for the floor, I clotheslined him, and I landed in an exhausted heap on the floor, winning the match and retaining the title.

Directly after the show we flew back to the States, where I was hosting *Sunday Night Heat* from the *World* in Times Square (the now-closed WWE restaurant). I had only gotten about two more hours of sleep and looked like a cadaver on TV. It wasn't pretty! The next night, November 5, 2001, I lost the I-C title (again) in Long Island to Test. My how far we'd come from our first encounter in Bret's poolroom.

It wouldn't be a long time until the ol' Edgemeister had gold around his waist again. The next week, on November 12, on *Raw* I beat Kurt Angle for the U.S. title at the Fleet Center in Boston. This set up a title-for-title unification match at the *Survivor Series* between Test and myself vying for the U.S. and I-C titles on November 18 in Greensboro, North Carolina.

The day of the match Test and I worked on the finish to our match. Test would go for his full nelson slam (or the "Uncle Slam" if you remember the Patriot) and I would roll forward and through for the pin. Sounds good on paper, but when I went to do it I landed right on my head! *Hard!* I was out of it for the rest of the day. Luckily our agent was Johnny Laurinitis, who always had great ideas for false finishes. I mentally blanked out a couple of times but the match still worked

> **I landed right on my head! <u>Hard!</u> I was out of it for the rest of the day.**

out great. Thankfully, Test and I have good chemistry in the ring. In my humble opinion (or maybe not so humble) it was the best match on the show. Test and I had gone from living in a basement in Calgary, to unifying two of the most prestigious titles ever in our business. This time we pulled off the finish, and I have to admit, holding up both of those title belts felt damn good! It was my fourth I-C title reign, and at that time, I was the last man to hold the U.S. title—before it was reinstated in 2003. That win was something I never would have dreamed of. By the next week it was all but forgotten on TV, but not by me. Both of those bad boys are framed and hang proudly on my office wall.

In the midst of all of this, Alanah and I finally found the time to get married. We both got swept up with all that was happening to me professionally without really thinking about whether this was a good idea or not. At this point I was definitely wearing rose-colored glasses.

My next angle was a complete departure from the feuds I had been involved in prior to this time in my career. His Lordship William Regal is one of my favorite people in the dressing room and was a good test for me. The European style of wrestling is more fluid. They have so many different moves that Regal knows, but when it comes to bumping he's the first to admit he is limited. After twenty-one years in the business, like Regal has had, you become limited to what bumps you can take. It took neck surgery for me to learn this. No more Ladder matches for me. Instead, you learn how to work. That involves your character. That is what Regal has. Natural heat, great facials, amazing acting ability, and arrogant ring mannerisms. You want to hate him. It's hard to believe he was once a mullet-haired babyface. It was a good contrast between our characters. Regal was the aristocratic British snob who looked down his nose at long-haired, leather-pants-wearin', smart-ass Canadians.

> It's hard to believe he was once a mullet-haired babyface.

The weeks before our PPV match at *Vengeance* in San Diego, Regal had been knocking everyone out with brass knuckles, including me.

> Regal and I clocked each other so hard I think we were trying to make up for the fact that the knuckles were rubber.

Sometimes Regal and I clocked each other so hard I think we were trying to make up for the fact that the knuckles were rubber.

I defended my title at *Vengeance*, and on the next *SmackDown!*, from Bakersfield, California, I "broke" Regal's nose with an Edgeacution on a chair. (Outside the ring he needed surgery for a deviated septum so we incorporated it into the story line.) This set

up a match at the *Royal Rumble* in Atlanta in January 2002. Regal used his power of the punch and took my I-C title. It would signify the last time I held that title for now, but hell, I got four runs with it. I would have been thrilled with only one!

Of course, now I was hell-bent on revenge, which led to a forgettable Brass Knuckles on a Pole match during *No Way Out* in Milwaukee. I believe this match was another first, but hopefully also a last. It wasn't for lack of trying, but the match did not work well. It was just a hard match to put together. The fans know that there won't be a pin until someone gets the knucks, so false finishes beforehand are useless. Once the knucks are down, how long can the match go before we use them? As we both crawled for the knucks Regal kicked them out of the ring. I went after them as he dug a second pair out of his trunks. One power of the punch later, Regal kept his title and I looked like a pretty dumb babyface. Just like the TLC matches, it's hard when a heel goes over in a blow-off match. It doesn't usually leave the 'face with much momentum. Originally we were slated to work *WrestleMania X8* in Toronto at the SkyDome. I would have won my fifth I-C title in the same building I won my first, but it was not in the cards. Regal went on to work Rob Van Dam and I went on to work Booker T.

Booker is a great wrestler and an all-around nice guy. I was really looking forward to working with him. Although I cannot say I was equally looking forward to the fact that our feud would be over a Japanese shampoo endorsement. Yes, you read

It may have been funny on paper but it played out like a fart in church.

that right. It may have been funny on paper but it played out like a fart in church. Everyone thought we needed a reason to fight each other, but no one wanted it to be set in the scenario where Booker costs me a match and then I cost him one in return, and the feud is born. Personally, I would have preferred that scenario, but we both tried to make the best of the situation. It still ended up being an amazing night for me. I was performing at *WrestleMania X8* in the SkyDome, twelve years after I sat fourteenth row ringside. My first solo 'Mania in front of over 68,000 hometown peeps. That was all the story we needed. I soaked it all in and I'll admit I had to fight back the tears. I will never forget that moment.

I had to keep it focused. After all, this was for the shampoo commercial.

The match itself was solid. Almost too solid. I was amped up and so was Booker. It was Booker's first *'Mania*, so it was hard not to be amped that night. I laced Booker with my first forearm shot and he wobbled. I thought it was a pretty good sell. Later, when we got to the back, I learned that I had wired the Bookerman on that first shot. He said he felt a shock down to his toes. Whoops! I guess that explains the wobble. Don't feel too sorry for Book though, because, trust me, he was also laying down some serious lumber out there. Watch it again, ignore the commentary and listen to the contact we were making. It had to be that way; we were fighting over shampoo, after all, and that is serious business. It was also nice to see one fan in the front row holding a sign emblazoned with "They are fighting over shampoo!" (Damn smart-ass Canadians!)

We were fighting over shampoo, after all, and that is serious business.

One thing I did learn that day is that even if an extremely white man (me) practices the Spinaroonie all day long, it still will not help. I don't even know if a month would've helped me. Although our time for the match had been cut back from fifteen minutes down to only eight ('Taker and Flair went way over before us) I was still blown sky high when it came time for my White-a-roonie. Some Caucasians should be banned from break dancing. I ended up with mat burns all over my arms and face. I took more punishment from my botched dance move than I did from Booker. Proving once again, without a shadow of a doubt, white men can't dance. At least not this one! Still, I was very pleased with the way it all turned out. My 'Mania record went to 3-0 after an Edgeacution allowing me to soak in the immensity of the crowd one more time. Little did I know that feeling would have to last, as this would be my last WrestleMania for a long time.

> **Some Caucasians should be banned from break dancing. I ended up with mat burns all over my arms and face.**

Shortly after *WrestleMania* it was decided to split the rosters and have two distinct brands. *Raw* on Mondays and *SmackDown!* on Thursdays. Separate story lines rarely interacting, essentially two different companies under one umbrella. The American League and the National League. It looked like a great opportunity for me to move up the card. It only made sense. If I was number ten on the totem pole and the five guys in front of me are suddenly gone, I am number five.

We did a draft for the top ten of each show. I was drafted number six on *SmackDown!* The Rock, Hulk Hogan, and Kurt Angle were at the top. Rock was going back to Hollywood, and Hulk was winding down. I looked at this as my opportunity to grab the damn ball out of someone's hands and take off. Luckily, I was about to be given that opportunity.

My opponent was Kurt Angle. Kurt is a natural, a pure phenom in our industry. I have never seen anyone become so good so fast, and probably never will again. In three short years he had accomplished literally everything in the business. Kurt's character was the perfect comic foil for my character outside of the ring, but more important, we became perfect opponents inside the ring as well.

The night after *WrestleMania* we started our angle (pun intended). I pinned Kurt in a tag match, on *Raw* from Montreal, pitting Kane and me against Kurt and Booker T. The next night, in Ottawa for our *SmackDown!* taping, Kurt cost me a match with Booker. A feud was born. Former friends in Team ECK, now fighting each other to make it to the top of *SmackDown!* We were setting up for a match at *Backlash,* yet along the way we also set up the forever immortalized "You suck" chant into Kurt's entrance music. And we ripped a page from the movie *Wayne's World* when I tried to "apologize" to Kurt. It

Anytime you can make fun of the male reproductive appendage on a worldwide scale it's a lot of fun!

was the first *SmackDown!* after the brand split from Rochester, New York, and Kurt and I were set to face off in singles action. In the spirit of friendship, I approached Kurt with some photos I had supposedly found in my attic. Each picture Kurt looked at had a different message written on the back with the arrows pointing up at him. "I'm a dork," "It's true, it's damn true!," and it kept going until the coup de grâce, "P.S.: I have no testicles!" with an arrow pointing down. Anytime you can make fun of the male reproductive appendage on a worldwide scale it's a lot of fun! As long as it's at someone else's expense, of course.

By the time *Backlash* rolled around I felt really good. I finally felt comfortable as a singles babyface and I was hitting my stride. *Backlash* further cemented that for me. The PPV took place in Kansas City and I had a good feeling throughout the day. I really felt like I was about to round a corner in my career. Kurt, John Laurinaitis (our agent), and I sat down and hammered out what turned into one hell of a match at *Backlash*. We had the crowd biting hard at our false finishes. One of the best feelings in the world to me is hearing the crowd count along with the pins. My favorite sequence happened when Kurt grabbed a chair and went to hit me with it. I moved and the chair ricocheted off the ropes into Kurt's head. I nailed the Edge-O-Matic (trust me, I have more brutal uses for the word *edge*) and Kurt kicked out at the very last nanosecond. I set up for the spear, but Kurt saw it coming and punted me into next week. He then followed it with his second Angle Slam and a one-two-three. But, fear not, dear reader, losing this match did more for me than winning ten matches could. This was only the beginning.

On *SmackDown!* the following week I came out to congratulate Kurt on the unveiling of his new T-shirt. Unbeknownst to him, I had replaced the shirt with a T-shirt that read "You Suck!" Of course I never saw any royalty checks from it. (You're a cheap bastard, Kurt.) But the look on his face was priceless when he realized what I had done!

Finally, the next week on *SmackDown!,* from his hometown of Pittsburgh, Kurt unveiled *his* T-shirt with guest model Lance Storm. It read "I've Got Gold, How 'Bout You?" Of course, I took this opportunity to

Immortalizing the chant that greets Kurt all over the world.

bring out my guest model, Val Venis (Sean) sporting the "You Suck" T-shirt. Kurt didn't appreciate that too much; he pretty much went ballistic and challenged me to a haircut match at *Judgment Day*. This idea was originally pitched for Jay (Christian) and me, but Jay balked (like me, he would look ugly bald, don't you think?). Being the trooper that he is, Kurt decided to do it. It ended up being a really entertaining angle that Kurt and I were both pleased with. The lead-up also marked the first time I would team with my childhood idol, Hulk Hogan.

We were in Bridgeport, Connecticut, where Hulk and I were set to take on Chris Jericho and Kurt. Before the match they aired a pretape of me walking into Hulk's dressing room and discovering his gear. Now, to a bona fide Hulkamaniac, this was like discovering the Holy Grail. I grabbed the "Hulk Rules" bandanna, the feather boa, looked into a mirror, and cut into some of my favorite Hogan promos that I had done so many times as a kid. "I've been hangin' and bangin' for forty days and forty nights on the *Titanic*, brother. I hopped on the back of a great white shark, grabbed it by its dorsal fin, with the largest arms . . . well, some pretty big arms, and said, 'Whatcha gonna do, brother!'" As I hit the most muscular pose, Hogan walked in, cut a "real" Hogan promo, and we left for the ring. That pretape is still the one I had the most fun doing! (But not to forget the fun I had with "Soda's Rule" with Mick and Christian making weight for the cruiser-weight title in a chicken suit!)

The Edgemeister does not take too kindly to getting hit with sledgehammers . . .

The match went very well. At the end of the match Triple H ran down and cleaned house with his sledgehammer. (He was going to be facing Jericho in a Hell in a Cell match at *Judgment Day*.) The Edgemeister does not take too kindly to getting hit with sledgehammers, so the next week I called him out, telling him I wanted to play "The Game." After throwing our punk cards in each other's faces we threw hands, chucked some knucks, got into a slobberknocker, the works. (Actually, we only threw about five punches before we were rudely interrupted and jumped by Kurt and Jericho.) Jericho held my arms and Kurt proceeded to cut a chunk out of my "hair like a lion" before we were through setting up our next tag team match, which was to take place at the end of the show.

In a pretape before the next match Triple H and I once again got into each other's faces. He told me to win some world titles before getting in his face. My response was that I could've taken his path and slept with the boss's daughter to get to the top. Ouch!

Letting Triple H know I was ready to play "The Game."

I really enjoy the chemistry Hunter and I have together, and along with 'Taker and Michaels, he is a guy I have always wanted to do singles business with. Maybe one day. But I digress, that night we had a tag team main event to take care of. As Jericho and Triple H fought to the back, I set up Kurt for the spear. He countered and laced me with a chair. All of this was followed by an Angle Slam and he pinned me. The last shot of the show, leading to the next PPV, was of Kurt dangling the chunk of my Japanese-shampooed hair over my unconscious face. Oh, the shit was on!

I was going to be bald! My head is shaped roughly the same as the Great Gazoo's green helmeted head from the _Flintstones_. It would not be a pretty sight.

When I got to the arena the day of the PPV in Nashville, I found out Kurt was going over. I was going to be bald! My head is shaped roughly the same as the Great Gazoo's green helmeted head from the _Flintstones_. It would not be a pretty sight. I assumed it was a rib since Vince and Shane seemed a little too interested in the outcome. We had about three hours until showtime, and I started to really believe Kurt was going over and I was going to be a bowling ball. Just before I got on a laptop backstage to order a hat from every NHL team in the

One . . . more . . . false finish.

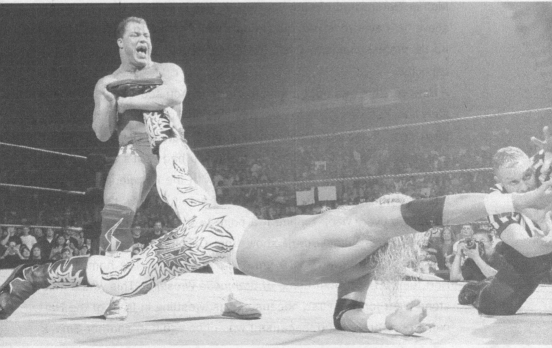

league, they let the cat out of the bag. Kurt was not going over, he was really the one going bald, which warranted many inner sighs of relief from me.

That night Kurt and I went out and had an awesome match. (It became a Match of the Year nominee.) We threw everything at each other. I think we actually had people believing Kurt was going to win at one point. Father Time was already in the lead to remove Kurt's hair, so it seemed obvious to some of the fans who was going over, but I think we overcame that obstacle. After about ten false finishes Kurt locked me in an ankle lock; as I neared the ropes he pulled me away to the middle of the ring. I spun and kicked him into the ropes. He bounced back into a small package and a one-two-three count later, Kurt Angle was going bald! Although not before he took off running, making me chase him around the building. Finally he jumped me and dragged me out to the barber's chair, leaving everyone wondering if I was really the one who would eventually lose my hair that night. No sir, not that night. I reversed things before it was too late and put Kurt in an old-school sleeper hold. Earlier in the day Kurt said he wanted me to lock it on good, so I did. Almost too good. Over the sound of the crowd I could barely make out Kurt sputtering "I can't breathe!" Whoops, I eased up on the sleeper and proceeded to finish what Mother Nature had already started. It wasn't exactly the smoothest shave he's ever received, but he survived. Thanks to this match and Kurt's professionalism, I felt like I had finally arrived in a singles capacity.

However, this was not the end to our feud. You see, according to the story line, Kurt was going to wear a toupee held on by amateur-wrestling head gear. It looked absolutely hilarious! Picture David Hasselhoff making a wig out of his chest hair and you had Kurt's toupee. Each week on commentary Tazz supplied us with the knowledge that Kurt had taken hair supplement products to help him grow his hair back faster! So every week I made it a point to try to take his wig off.

Finally, on a *SmackDown!* show from Calgary, Kurt and I had our blow off. A Cage match in a great wrestling town. The home of the Hart family. The former home of *Stampede Wrestling*. This was a milestone night for me. First, because I was wrestling in front of the Hart patriarch, Stu. Second, because I was once again in another *Smack-*

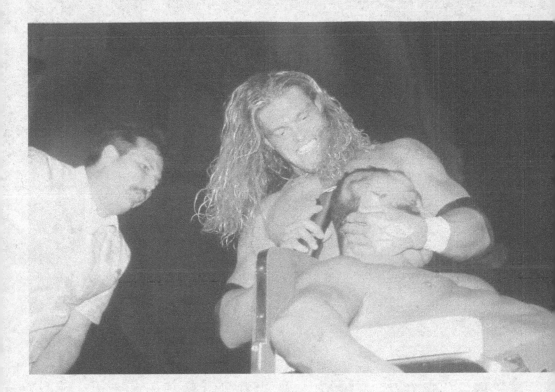

Down! main event. Third, because I was ending my most successful singles program to date, and fourth but not least, because I was blading for the first time. I always said I wouldn't blade until it meant something. Not until I was in a great angle or until it would possibly add something to the match. This was the perfect opportunity to break my gigging cherry! I broke it . . . a little too much. I ended up gigging for five or six stitches. Hey, I wanted to make sure I did it right. Obviously I went too deep, making me look like Sissy Spacek at the end of *Carrie*. Kurt and I engaged in what might be my best match to date. He Angle Slammed me from the top rope. I used his ankle lock and Angle Slam. It went on and on. Even my man the Hulkster came out to help, which set him and Angle up for the next *King of the Ring*. There was my childhood hero helping me! Cheering me on, in Calgary, Alberta, Canada! All the ingredients were there for a major goose-bump moment. The moment didn't last long, though. The match was nearing its end. I was perched on the top rope like a vulture, covered in blood. Kurt was across the ring snorting like a wig-wearing bull and my ass was the matador's cape. We planned this out to look like two warriors charging head-on at the end of a long battle. Two rams col-

What does he have this thing on with?

liding. Apollo Creed and Balboa at the end of *Rocky III*. Kurt charged and I speared his head off from the top rope. My problem was the landing. I had never really factored in that part until I landed straight down on my elbow and felt my shoulder pop. My arm immediately went

All the ingredients were there for a major goose bump moment.

numb and limp. I rolled on top and as the crowd counted one-two-three with referee Brian Hebner, I was worried. Just as I was cementing a single, main

event spot, I did something painfully wrong to my shoulder. Even worse, I had to get up and pose in an after-match celebration. Normally, I would have said no and beaten it to the back, but this was not your average after-match pose. This pose was with Hulk Hogan! As a kid I posed with Hogan numerous times when he was on TV, but now I had a chance to pose beside him. Busted head and torn shoulder, I was posing no matter what. Every time I did a pose my shoulder popped, but I had that big cheesy grin on my face the whole time. Hulk knew how much I enjoyed doing that bit. I had filled him in earlier about my childhood obsession. Never did I think he and I would be peers, in the same company, at the same time! I have to admit, it was another childhood dream of mine being fulfilled on that show. And once again, Kurt and I gave our all for one hell of a performance.

Amazing . . . getting to pose in the ring with Hulk Hogan.

CHAPTER

After the match it was time to get stitches and lick my wounds. I just wanted to go back to my hotel room and relax, but Jericho and some of the other guys had other ideas. They wanted to celebrate with a night on the town. Hell, even anti-party-animal Lance was going, and I couldn't let him show me up! I got my stitches done and finally had some movement in my arm again, so I decided to celebrate my milestone night. I had fun, but paid for it the next day when I couldn't lift my arm.

I was already scheduled to fly to Toronto to visit my ma, but I had to make a stop first to see the Toronto Maple Leafs team doctor. After talking to him and doing some arm movements he scheduled me for an MRI the following day. I'd had MRI's done before, but this one was different. They took a seven-inch needle that looked like a flagpole and stuck it into my shoulder joint. After injecting dye into the joint I had to contort my body into a certain, and very uncomfortable, position to get the proper view to see what was going on. MRI machines are not built for large people, and I had no choice but to lay there with my arm bent behind my head for about half an hour.

"Huh? I don't have a labia!"

The results were worse than the procedure. When I went back to the doctor's office he told me I had a torn labrum. "Huh? I don't have a labia!" Yeah, I was right. I didn't have a labia, but I did indeed have a labrum. The doctor then explained that I had a sizable tear that would require surgery to correct. To add insult to injury, after the surgery I would have to endure at least six months of rehab. I couldn't believe it! Injuries are never good, but this felt like the worst possible timing. I am usually a pretty positive guy, but this news had me depressed and a bit stressed out.

Unfortunately WWE doesn't stop for injuries. The show must go on.

The writers and I came up with an idea to explain my absence. A novel idea! Tell the truth! I had a *King of the Ring* qualifying match where I would be defending my throne against Chris Jericho. I came out in street clothes with my arm in its sling and cut a very real promo. It was me and it was how I felt. There was no hiding the frustration I felt. I couldn't hide the fact that I was pissed off. Pissed off at my body for giving out on me, and I said so. The company had finally handed me the ball and now I couldn't even hold it. That was how I truly felt. In some ways it was almost therapeutic to be able to say it out loud and in front of that many people. Originally, I was set to go to the finals and face Brock Lesnar, instead I had to forfeit my match with Chris.

Before the injury Jericho and I were about to start a new program, so it was decided he would get the heat for the shoulder injury. After I finished my promo his music hit, he came out and attacked the injured shoulder. He set my shoulder over the ring stairs and slammed a chair right on the joint. When we finished the night's business I assumed I would be off the show for at least six months—that is, until I went to see Dr. James Andrews in Birmingham, Alabama.

He had a different prognosis. For Dr. Andrews surgery was the last resort. He said I would eventually need surgery to correct the problem, but he suggested I try rehabing it first for a month and see how it held up. After a month of strict rehab, if it didn't get any better I would have to go under the knife, which I had eluded so far. Six days a week, two hours a day, I rehabbed my right shoulder. From there I would go to the gym to continue training my healthy left side. Slowly I incorporated the right side and added weights. Three weeks later I was ready to come back better than ever and pick up where I left off. Or so I was hoping.

> After a month of strict rehab, if it didn't get any better I would have to go under the knife . . .

I busted my ass to make sure my comeback could take place at the All State Arena in Chicago. It is one of my favorite buildings and always hosts an amazing crowd. That night on *SmackDown!* the main event was Jericho vs. Hulk. Jericho blasted Hulk with a chair and set him up on the stairs for the same shoulder-injuring chair shot he had so eloquently delivered to me a month before.

I had come up with an idea that I brainstormed with Jericho and Paul Heyman for the comeback. I wanted Jericho's music to hit right before he creamed Hulk with the chair. With the cue of his music, I would come out while the lights were off and hit his trademark pose at the top of the ramp. We did it and it worked out great. I slowly turned, spit out my gum (à la Jericho), and charged the ring.

In my time off I had bought some new "character clothes." Clothes I wouldn't wear anywhere else but on TV. They were great clothes for my character but not the best clothes for the action my character had to endure. As I ran down the ramp and slid into the ring ready to conquer the world, my new pants blew out in the crotch. No problem, right? Wrong! The problem here, people, was that I was flying commando, not even a wing man. No underwear, no boxers, no banana hammocks, nothing underneath. My boys were out there. The pants rode low on my waist, and since flashing your Calvin Kleins went out with Marky Mark and the Funky Bunch I opted for my birthday britches! So now, instead of worrying about my Calvins hanging out I was worried something else might be hanging out. I learned a new style of wrestling that night, and very carefully beat the hell out of Jericho all the while making sure my package stayed in the cockpit. Talk about a wardrobe malfunction! I made it through the run-in without any censorship and Jericho took off, leaving me to once again pose with the Hulkster. When I got backstage I told Vince he may need to edit my near testicle side show, giving him a good chuckle but more importantly giving me my comeback!

As I ran down the ramp and slid into the ring . . . my new pants blew out in the crotch . . . The problem here, people, was that I was flying commando, not even a wing man . . . My boys were out there.

Jericho and I geared up for what we were told would be a three-month program, culminating in one of two scenarios. A Cage match at *SummerSlam* or Jericho with his band, Fozzy, in one corner against me and Ozzy Osbourne in my corner. Obviously and regrettably, that never materialized, and neither did our program. Instead, I started teaming with Hulk. Our crowd knew my history and the team worked. With the interaction Hulk and I had done so far I think the company realized it had something. When something works, you run with it. The chemistry was there and the people latched on to it. I was stoked for teaming with Hulk and it meant less punishment and bumps for him. That would be my job. We teamed the next week to face Billy and Chuck for the tag team titles in Boston. It would air on the Fourth of July edition on *SmackDown!* We taped the match on July 2, 2002. Nine years and one day into my career.

Hulk came out to the ring that night with his old Real American theme song. It was the first and only time he did that in his comeback. They got a shot of me and I was beaming like Pete Rose holding a winning ten-team parley ticket from Caesar's Sports Book. I felt like a kid again. Every emotion you saw that night was one hundred percent real. Hulk was real easy to team with. He said to me, "Just tell me what you want me to do, brother!" I came up with an idea to do a double boot, followed by a double leg drop. The classic Hogan one-two combination. I threw it out there and he dug it. After hitting our leg drops we were the new Tag Team Champions! It was my eighth tag

title win, only this one was with the icon I grew up watching. It was his first WWE Tag Team title. What a memory.

On July 4, I went to his place for a day of Sea-dooing and BBQ. Later that night we watched the match on *SmackDown!* before I went home. Critics can scoff but I never thought, while I was sitting in my ma's old rocking chair, that some twenty years later I would be sitting with Hulk Hogan and watching us win the tag team title. Years from now I will watch that and still have a smile on my face.

I never thought . . . that some twenty years later I would be sitting with Hulk Hogan and watching us win the tag team title. Years from now I will watch that and still have a smile on my face.

It was only a short-term run with the tag title. We were what you call transitional champions. We were used to get the titles in the hands of the Un-Americans, Jay (Christian) and Lance Storm during *Vengeance* in Detroit, July 2002. (That three-week run with the title was the most fun I have had in the business.) The match at *Vengeance* proved to be a good one. We didn't have as much time as we would've liked to have had, but the finale worked well. After run-ins by Test and Rikishi, Jericho came through the crowd and whacked me with the title belt. Ironically giving Jay his eighth tag title win and Lance his first.

Jericho and I were back on track, but just as he hopped back on the rug it was pulled out from under us again. It was decided that Chris and the Un-Americans were going to jump ship and head to *Raw*. *Raw* needed some help, so Jericho and I had to blow off our feud a week after *Vengeance* in Indianapolis on *SmackDown!* We were both upset, feeling as though there was money to be made on our angle, only it was blown off in one match. At least it was a Cage match, which was slowly replacing the Ladder match for me (the lesser of two evils?).

This match is still among my favorites. The first real test for the torn shoulder ligament came after a bulldog off the top rope. It hurt like hell, but held up. We used the over-the-top escape for the finish. It's never as gratifying for the crowd as a pin, but as he crawled for the door, I climbed over for the win and it worked. Before I could bask in my victory, I was jumped by the Un-Americans, who threw me back into the cozy confines of the steel cage. Four Canadians against one,

Chris, holding on isn't going to save you.

beating me down as if I had stolen their last Labatt's Blue. Rey Mysterio, who made his WWE debut that night, came down and hit a dive from the top of the cage. Vanilla white meat babyface John Cena came down, too, and the three of us ran the rascally Canadians off to *Raw*.

But before they ran off, we had a trip to Australia, which had already been advertised. I would wrestle Jericho again in front of my third largest crowd. There were 56,700 screaming Aussies in Melbourne ready to see WWE for the first time in a decade. It was fun and the crowd was rabid with their lively chants of "Jericho's a wanker!" After the match I was still amped up, so I climbed the lighting truss high above the crowd—another career highlight. The Aussie Edgeheads were true class acts. Our angle ended there and was now officially done. It was time for my next opponent.

"Jericho's a wanker!"

W ith the departure of Jericho and the Un-Americans, *SmackDown!* got Chris Benoit and Eddie Guerrero. Two absolute artists in the ring. Their first match on *SmackDown!* was in the main event against The Rock and me. Since Jericho and I were scrapped, the new game plan was that I would work Benoit at *SummerSlam* for the I-C title. In the end, Benoit worked RVD and dropped the title to get it back to *Raw.* With the story line changed once again, I ended up wrestling Eddie. Either way I had a win-win situation.

The week before the PPV, Rock and I teamed against Eddie and Benoit for a second time. I speared Eddie for the pin in order to help create some build up between Eddie and myself. Not much for the fans to bite into, but when it came to match time we wanted to give

them something to chew on. However, we both came away from that match disappointed. We knew we could pull a better match out of each other. During the match we worked my still injured shoulder, but at that point the audience had forgotten all about it. The drama for the spear and desperate babyface win was just not where he and I wanted it to be. The ol' Vin man was not impressed with the match either. Like us, he expected more. It became a work in progress. Our matches against each other were good, just not great. We wrestled each other in tag team matches with assorted partners, where I had been the orchestrator in two Guerrero Stinkfaces leading up to our *Unforgiven* match in Los Angeles.

During a Six Man Tag match with Undertaker, Rikishi, and myself against Eddie, Kurt, and Benoit, I shoved Eddie's face so far up Rikishi's ample rump that he was tickling his tonsils. The following week, I inserted Eddie's face into his nephew Chavo Guerrero's gluteus maximus. Poor Eddie, he's a true pro so I felt bad doing it. Eddie ended up getting his revenge on me, so I didn't feel bad for too long. Eddie came back to blast me in the head with a sick-looking chair shot, busting me open like a cherry tomato. Because of this story line I was walking into the match with a concussion. Concussion or not, it gave us a lot more of a buildup for our match at *Unforgiven* and it helped bring our match up a notch. Still, it fell below our expectations. During the match Eddie exposed a turnbuckle. Eventually we were in that corner for an Edgemeister superplex. Eddie followed this up by ramming my concussed head into the steel buckle, teamed with an incredibly fast sunset powerbomb that looked as if it gave me a real concussion.

> I shoved Eddie's face so far up Rikishi's ample rump that he was tickling his tonsils. . . . Poor Eddie, he's a true pro so I felt bad doing it. Eddie ended up getting his revenge on me . . .

The next night I wrestled Brock Lesnar during one of the live events in Santa Barbara, California. We'd been working the main events on the live shows for the past couple of months and had good chemistry from the first night. Sometimes it just works out that way. You never know who you are going to click with businesswise, but this seemed to be working.

It was a busy couple of days. After my bouts with Eddie and Brock

Eddie shows his Latino heat.

there was still more work to be done. Kurt, Torrie Wilson, Brock, and I took a WWE jet to Seattle that night for the *WrestleMania* press conference that was being held the following day. We got into Seattle very late and didn't get to bed until five A.M. It felt like no sooner did I shut my eyes than the wake-up call came, and I was up at eight A.M. getting ready for another long day. We were all running on low fuel but still made it to the press conference on time. When the press conference was finished we all hopped on the plane and flew south to San Diego for our *SmackDown!* taping. When I arrived at the arena later that afternoon, exhausted, I found out I had to wrestle in a twenty-minute No Disqualification match against Eddie Guerrero. That, my friends, is the life of a wrestler. Exhausted or not I was determined to have a good match with Eddie. This was it. We were going to get "it" that night, I just felt it in the air.

I hope I don't come across as an egomaniac, but that night Eddie and I found "it," we tore it up. We only had two spots set and did the rest of the match on the fly. We were in a zone. At one juncture I went to blast Eddie with a ladder (yes, the ladder rears its ugly head again!) but he ducked and our referee, Mike Sparks, ate a steel sandwich. I

> *I hope I don't come across as an egomaniac, but that night Eddie and I found "it"...*

217

think this match may have accelerated the problems with my neck. Eddie had given me a forearm uppercut bumping me back first onto a ladder. My neck landed on a rung and I heard it pop. Now, I don't think that broke it, but it definitely did not help matters. As I lay beaten on top of one ladder, Eddie proceeded to put another ladder on top of me crunching me between the two with a ladder Malachi crunch (*Happy Days*, remember?). This move actually put me on the brink of unconsciousness. When Eddie hit his rolling hilo, the ladder on top of me slammed off my temple. Eddie covered me, although at that moment I didn't know if I would be able to even kick out. I probably should have stayed down, but I couldn't. Glutton for punishment, I

Oh yeah, I am a rocket scientist! We hit the move perfectly except for the fact that my head was whiplashed off the canvas. As I laid there I said to myself, "What in the hell was I thinking?"

very stupidly got up. In the meantime, Eddie had scaled a ladder to hit his Frog Splash. I followed suit and climbed the other side as we fought back and forth to the top of the ladder. Right around this time Eddie turned up his Latino Heat, scorching the hell out of me. Eddie started ramming my head into the top of the ladder, followed by a move that caused me to not be able to turn my head for three days. It was my idea, so I had no one to call a dumb ass but me. Eddie hit me with the same sunset flip powerbomb he connected with two nights earlier. Only this time it was elevated from the top of the ladder. Oh yeah, I am a rocket scientist! We hit the move perfectly except for the fact that my head was whiplashed off the canvas. As I laid there I said to myself, "What in the hell was I thinking?" I would have thought I was completely crazy at that point until I heard the roar of the crowd. "Oh yeah, that was what I was thinking!" As Eddie crawled over to me I heard him say, "We got 'em now, baby!" Damn straight we did!

Normally that would have been the finish, but this was our blow-off. We protected the move with time before the cover and I was the proverbial babyface in peril. I kicked out on a two-and-three-quarter count, then a very strange thing started to happen. The crowd was cheering us both. They were on their feet cheering our match, but it wasn't over yet. I back dropped Eddie into a ladder, making him ricochet off, landing him directly on his head. Eddie definitely felt that one. I remember him saying "Launch me, baby!" so I did, but I knew it would be an ugly landing. There was no way for it not to hurt, but Eddie's a trooper. After I got the referee Mike Chioda to make sure he was alive and somewhat well, I climbed a ladder that I had set up in the opposite corner. Eddie somehow pulled himself to his feet and met me once again at the top of the ladder. Only this time my Canadiano Heat sent flames in his direction. I took his head and violently rammed it off the top of the ladder. On the third or fourth teeth-rattling noggin-knocker I heard "Okay, that's good!" not realizing I had delivered a cranium cracker that opened him up for nine stitches and one huge lump on his forehead. We were nearing the light at the end of the tunnel. The light was shining bright even though we had beaten ourselves into near incoherence. Still on top of the ladder, I hooked Eddie for an Edgeacution as the crowd anticipated that something sick was about to happen. The crowd gasped as I hit my finisher off the top of the ladder. Bam! We hit the mat, allowing me to drape myself across Eddie for the one-two-three count. What the hell else could we do? The crowd was once again on their feet giving us both a standing ovation. It's strange when a heel struggles to his feet and receives a standing O, but Eddie got it and it was very much deserved.

It was a pleasure to hear that San Diego crowd. It was a pleasure to be in that match, and it was a pleasure and a privilege to wrestle Eddie Guerrero. It was not a pleasure, however, getting up the next day and flying

I still get goose bumps when I watch that match. Thank you, Eddie!

home. Eddie and I were on the same flight and it was not pretty. The lump and nine stitches on Eddie's forehead made him look like a Mexican Elephant Man. His shoulders were slumped and I could tell every move he made hurt. I couldn't turn my head and knew what he was going through. Eddie walked like Quasimodo and I was doing my best impression of Frankenstein. Come to think of it, it definitely felt like I had bolts in my neck (but that comes later). I have a feeling this match, along with some of the other Ladder matches, sped along the deterioration of my neck. We paid the price but we fought a great fight. Call me a sadist if you want, but I still get goose bumps when I watch that match. Thank you, Eddie!

Things on the home front were on shaky ground. They had been for a long time, but I had tried to set that notion aside. Problems would surface, but we never really solved them before it was time for me to go on the road again. That's not to say my job was one of the problems. A strong couple can work through anything, plain and simple. It was a work in progress, but at least I was finally able to relax at home, though not for long. I laid in bed for about three days until I was able to turn my head, then it was time to hit the road again.

Coming off my last match with Eddie and still recovering, I was hoping my next assignment would be a little more forgiving on the ol' bod. No such luck. I was set to work Kurt Angle. Kurt is a joy to wrestle but he just keeps coming. He forces the best out of you, even if you feel like you have nothing left. This night was not different. I hit Kurt with the

Oh well, that's our business. We have to work through our pain.

spear for the win, but in doing so I also jammed my wrist. It hurt like hell, but I kept it to myself and started to heavily tape it after that match. Just like the unknown fracture I had in my skull, I later found out I had fractured my wrist. Oh well, that's our business. We have to work through our pain.

Finishing the weekend of live shows we were off to Lafayette, Louisana, for *SmackDown!* I pulled the Angle card again, so I knew it would not be an easy night. We went for twenty-five very long minutes. We had double pins, two referees fighting, and an appearance by Chris Benoit. I give everything I have any time that you see me, but Kurt and I were firing on all cylinders that night when we faced each other. That's just how it was with us. I would like you to believe that anytime you saw Edge/Kurt on the bill you were going to get your money's worth. It's a forgotten match, but it's another one of my personal favorites (Kurt ended up in quite a few of my personal favorites).

A new tag team was made. Edge & Rey Mysterio. Now I knew I was gonna have some fun.

Things were definitely looking up for the Edger, but I was running out of top-level opponents and story lines. Every time this happens I get put in a tag team. Tag teams are one thing I do well, but it does get frustrating. As well as I was rolling, I still wanted to transform the live events I was working with Brock into a PPV angle. They didn't want to go in that direction. Brock was wrestling 'Taker, so a new tag team was made. Edge & Rey Mysterio. Now I knew I was gonna have some fun.

Rey and I are great friends outside the ring. We had teamed together once to close down the New Haven Coliseum. Our styles are completely opposite, yet somehow we complement each other. Neither one of us had opponents, so it only seemed natural. A new tag team was formed.

A tournament was set to crown the first ever *SmackDown!* tag team champions. The plan was for Rey and me to go through to the finals to face Angle and Benoit. Tag team wrestling was about to take a big step up on *SmackDown!*

The tournament started in Phoenix with Rey and me beating Brock and Tajiri in the main event. The second round of the tournament took place in Toronto at the ACC in what I remember to be one of the loudest reactions I had ever received. This was also the first time my grandparents would see me wrestle in person for WWE.

It's amazing how things can come full circle. A decade after my grandpa would drive me down to wrestling classes, he found himself sitting in a packed house in Toronto watching his grandson wrestle with his and my grandma's initials adorned on my wrist tape. I know my grandma winces when I take punishment in the ring, but my mom said she did okay that night and warned her when the pyro would go off, bless her little heart (now I can say it to her). I wouldn't be where I am without them, so it was a special night for me to have them there.

Rey and I had a short match that night in Toronto against D-Von and Ron Simmons, and we took care of business, marching ourselves right into the finals. Angle and Benoit defeated the Guerrero boys and the stage was set. It would be the four of us in the tag team finals at *No Mercy*.

No Mercy was in Little Rock, Arkansas, that year on October 20, 2002. Fans pegged it to be a classic, but that didn't guarantee it would be. We got our strategy together beforehand and put in everything we could fit until it was busting at the seams. It was a roller coaster. This match was just fun to be a part of. I think I threw Rey around as much as Kurt and Benoit did. Kurt delivered the finish by making me tap

It was a roller coaster. This match was just fun to be a part of.

to the ankle lock. I've never been the kind of babyface who worries about losing clean. I think that has been proven before and will be proven again many more times. As long as the match was great, that's what the fans remember. At the time, some said this may have been the best WWE Tag Team match ever; it was voted match of the year. Personally, I knew it was good and special, but let's not overdo it! Someone else's best may be another's worst. It's too subjective. Who knows who or what is truly the best of all time in anything? The crowd walked away entertained that night and that is really all that matters.

Who knows who or what is truly the best of all time in anything?

Now there were three teams all vying for the tag team titles. Rey and myself, Kurt with Benoit, and the Guerreros. Each week, whether it was tags or singles, it was a combination of the six of us. The series really gave Chavo Guerrero a chance to show what he could do, and we got some really good wrestling accomplished. Our feud continued on a whirlwind European tour through Finland, Ireland, a PPV in Manchester (where I wrestled my first PPV main event versus Brock Lesnar and Paul Heyman), and ended in Sheffield.

When we got back to the States we were booked on *SmackDown!* in a Two Out of Three Falls tag match with Angle and Benoit. We were in Manchester again, only this was Manchester, New Hampshire. Before that match even began I had an eighteen-minute Triple Threat match with Eddie and Benoit for a special on UPN during sweeps

It doesn't matter how short our reign was, a win is a win.

week. That is a night's work in itself, but Benoit and I still had the thirty-minute main event Two Out of Three Falls match.

With Rey as a partner every match is fun, and this match was no exception. We ended up winning the *SmackDown!* Tag Team Championships, bringing my total to nine with three different partners. Our reign would be short-lived—two weeks to be exact. We had a Three Team Elimination match during *Survivor Series* on November 17, 2002, in Madison Square Garden. None of us were all that happy with this match. It felt rushed and we eliminated that night's crowd favorites, Benoit and Angle first. Ending the match by dropping the titles to the Guerreros pretty much ended my team with Rey, but it was fun while it lasted.

in it, but it did add drama to the match. We may have even broken the record for false finishes in this match, and the fans in Dallas ate it all up, smacking their lips for more. Finally, I tried to hobble to the top rope, where Kurt caught me with a brutal Angle Slam off the top for the win.

I had survived and was given time off to recuperate. But this little bit of time off didn't help my healing process much. I was due in Fort Lauderdale for *Armageddon* to face the newly christened A-Train and I was still in a lot of pain.

I pitched the idea for the feud to take place with Matt Hardy. He was set to attack my knee in Dallas and during the following matches he could do most of the running to help me work around my injury. Instead, A-Train was plucked out of a year's worth of *Velocity* matches and added to the mix. It was a complicated situation for both of us to be put in. People didn't have enough time to care about A-Train or what he was about. Most fans hadn't seen or heard of him for the last year, and my work was rapidly going downhill. Working with A-Train I would be doing most of the running and bumping. The mark of a great worker is being able to pull it off, and that night I didn't. My performance and the match were not good. I got some criticism from Vince on this one. The perfectionist and drive in me always wants to steal the show and when I don't I accept full blame.

> The perfectionist and drive in me always wants to steal the show and when I don't I accept full blame.

I felt as though we redeemed ourselves a little the following week on *SmackDown!* from Tampa. We had a good match that was actually seen by more people than the week prior. A-Train is one hell of a working big man and we ended up having some good matches, much improved from the first. Still, it wasn't my best stuff. The knee injury was still slowing me down. Now it's time for the most overused cliché in our industry about an injury: "Hey, it ain't ballet." This, of course, is true, but essentially it means that wrestlers are tough and ballet dancers are not. This comment will continue to be used until one of us is surrounded in a hotel parking lot by a posse of ballet dancers and said wrestler has to eat a flurry of leotard-covered dropkicks. (Sorry, I got sidetracked.) Back to my roll call of injuries. Thankfully the days off in between added a little help to the situation, for my knee anyway. But there was something else nagging at me, something I kept trying to push away and not worry about. That something was neck pain.

The neck pain was a bad sign and it would not go away. Working Show and Train I was taking some big bumps while trying to avoid hurting my knee any more than it already was. To compensate for my knee, my neck started taking more punishment and wasn't ready for the extra pressure. I

> I dodged bullets with my shoulder and knee but my neck was in the crosshairs and I got hit dead center.

guess it was a culmination of eleven years of abuse and strain, meaning this was the end of the line. After all of the bumps from ladders, chairs, cages, the nights of sleeping in cars and on planes or even pencil-thin blue mats on hardwood floors it just all caught up with me. I dodged bullets with my shoulder and knee but my neck was in the crosshairs and I got hit dead center. I kept trying to ignore the pain, thinking eventually it would go away. I would get massages or have a chiropractor adjust me every chance I got, but nothing seemed to help. All it did was make me feel sick to my stomach. During my matches I'd take bumps and feel nauseous. My fingers started to tingle at one point. One night in Philly, Train forearmed me in the back and I lost feeling in both of my arms. I would touch the center of my palm and my hand would go numb. Meanwhile, I kept working and the neck pain kept getting worse. This went on for close to two months until one day in San Francisco the "man upstairs" sent me a major warning signal. I was at the gym training biceps. It was the day of a live event where I would be working Train once again. As I was curling I felt the strength in my left arm almost leave entirely. My right arm seemed fine, but I couldn't even force three reps with my left. Something was definitely wrong. I had traveled with Rhyno when he had neck problems and the symptoms seemed uncomfortably similar. I still managed to do the show, and later I made my way over to Bakersfield for our next match.

Once I got to Bakersfield I sat down with Benoit for a little heart to heart. We compared notes and came to the conclusion that I could be suffering from nerve damage caused by pressure on my spinal cord. It was the same thing that had happened to him. I finally told the office—Benoit was insistent—and got an MRI scheduled for when I got back home to Tampa. As you could imagine, the results of the MRI were not what I wanted to hear. The doctor told me that if I were to take another fall in the ring I could possibly end up in a wheelchair. Wow, that took the breath out of me. My mind was struggling to make sense of what he was saying. It was struggling even harder to accept what he was saying. He continued to tell me that my spinal cord was being significantly pinched and strongly suggested I get nowhere near a wrestling ring. I could not believe my ears, what was I going to do? I was scheduled at *No Way Out* in Montreal, teaming me with Brock and Benoit against Kurt and Team Angle. Of course, being the stubborn ass that I am, I decided I would be able to wrestle, but the office wanted me to get a second opinion from Dr. Lloyd Youngblood. Youngblood is a renowned surgeon who had fused the degenerated necks of six WWE Superstars. He was my last hope. Dr. Youngblood understood our industry, surely he'd tell me I was clear to wrestle in the six-man at *No Way Out*. Just a little rehab, right? Wrong!

I was wrong and never wanted to be more right in my life. Dr. Youngblood told me the exact same thing the other doctor had told me. My world was officially upside down. Everything I worked so hard for over the last eleven years was coming to a head and life on the home front wasn't going so great either. Everything personal and professional was spiraling downhill. The only positive thing in my eyes was the fact that I only needed two levels of my neck fused: C-5, C-6, and C-7. Bad, but the first doctor told me I may need to have three levels fused, which would have ended my career. Two levels is the limit. At twenty-nine I was facing spine surgery or risking paralysis. My mind was reeling. So many thoughts flashed through my mind. What if I could never wrestle again? What if I had to learn a whole new way of life? I want kids some day and all I could think of was how it

> **The doctor told me that if I were to take another fall in the ring I could possibly end up in a wheelchair. Wow, that took the breath out of me.**

229

could affect my unborn children. Would I be able to play with them, or simply hold them in my arms? So many thoughts traveled through my mind it was overwhelming. I still wanted to work, but Vince decided it wasn't a chance to take, so I was pulled from the six-man match at *No Way Out*. Now I had no way out of the surgery. I had to get it done and get healthy.

Before any of this had come about, I was advertised on a tour in South Africa, so I followed through on that commitment first. We postponed the surgery and I flew eighteen hours to South Africa with a broken neck. The flight really sucked but the tour of South Africa was a great experience.

My left arm had begun to atrophy. It looked as though someone had taken driving practice with an eight iron off my shoulder. My tricep had almost completely disappeared and no matter how hard I tried to flex it, it remained as soft as a pillow.

Each night of the South African tour I would come out to the ring and explain why I couldn't wrestle. The first night they even had Bill DeMott come out to get in my face and attack me. Bill kicked me in the stomach. I sold the kick like I normally would have, only with this kick I completely lost all of the feeling in my left arm. I dropped to my knees looking at my arm thinking, "Please come back!" Eventually, it did. I finished the tour without any other physical problems. The last night of the tour Matt, Rey, and some of the guys took me out for a little send-off party. By the end of the night Matt and I had transformed into our alter egos, Caveman Edge and Caveman Hardy. Matt always eats his food like a caveman, but when he drinks he looks the part, too. I had a good time and was glad I was able to go out for one last brew-ha-ha before my surgery, although it made me realize how much I was going to miss the boys.

I got back to Tampa and was able to rest for a week before the surgery, which took place on March 10, 2003, in San Antonio, Texas. The doctor explained how the surgery was going to go and surprisingly I was okay with it. Even after I signed the waiver stating that if I should die on the operating table Dr. Youngblood and the hospital were not responsible, I still felt pretty good. I had the utmost confidence in Dr. Youngblood. He made me feel at ease. He even patted

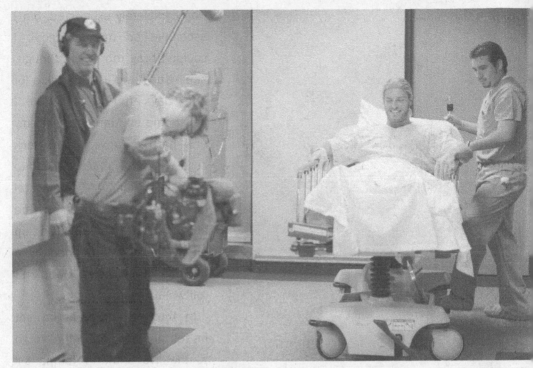

Doesn't everyone have a camera crew and a photographer follow them into surgery?

my hand as I went under and said, "We're going to get you back in the ring again, son." That was the last thing I remember.

The procedure was scheduled to take about three and a half hours but there were complications. My two discs were not just herniated, they were ruptured. This meant the bits of ruptured bone needed to be cleared out. After that, what was left of the disc would be drilled out. They started the surgery by making an incision in the front of my neck and moving my throat over three inches. After drilling out the discs, they filled them with bone that was removed from my hip. Following that, the doctor placed a titanium plate on the front of my spine that is held in place by six screws and six anchors that were drilled into the back of my spine.

The recovery time for the surgery is at least a year, and in some cases even longer, before you get medical clearance to step foot in the ring again. I had some good initial signs. Chris Benoit and Lita did flights of stairs the day of their surgeries, meaning of course, I had to do more. I ended up doing one hundred sixty flights of stairs and

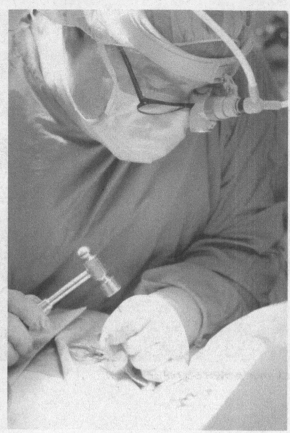
Dr. Youngblood working on me.

was completely exhausted, but I accomplished my first goal! I couldn't brag too much, though, seeing as how I lost my voice for a few days after the procedure. I flew home on March 13 with my new partner (a very hard neck collar) set firmly in place. I had to wear the collar 24/7 for a total of six weeks, except in the shower. I had to sleep sitting up on my couch surrounded by a fortress of pillows so I wouldn't roll while I slept.

In the meantime, I had set myself another goal. I had to go to the live show in Tampa six days after my surgery. It turned out to be a very long night, but I pulled it off. I even walked out to the ring with Rhyno, neck brace and all. My body let me know it didn't appreciate the early return when I got home that night, but it was worth it.

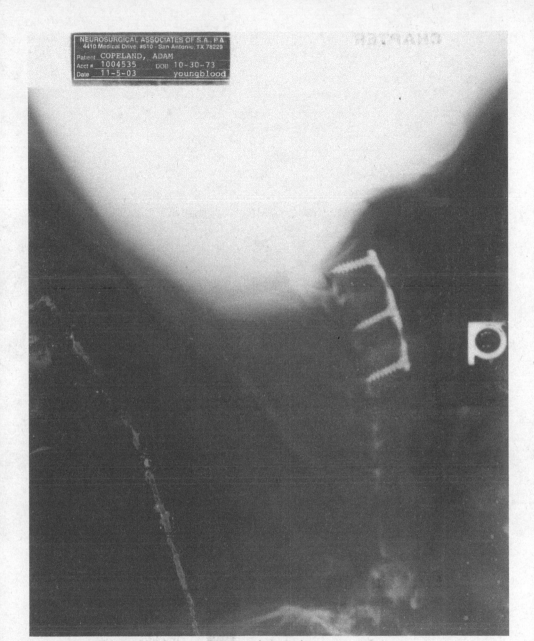

The neck of a professional wrestler.

In my fortress
of pillows.
That's Rhyno in
the nightgown.
Don't ask.

Luckily, my stubbornness comes in handy sometimes and I didn't give up.

The surgery was only the beginning of what felt like the longest year of my life.

I began working out again four weeks after the surgery. At the time, the goal of one day getting back into wrestling shape felt insurmountable. I could only lift two- to five-pound dumbbells—my hands were bigger than the weights. It was very limiting and pretty damn discouraging. After my first workout I felt like giving up. Luckily, my stubbornness comes in handy sometimes and I didn't give up.

In the first few months of my recovery phase, I kept myself as busy as I possibly could. I started writing this book you are now reading. I also began a column on WWE.com called the "Edgeucation of Adam Copeland" (a name the Hurricane came up with, which was also my personal choice for the title of this book).

Christmas at my mother's house. I had a little trouble getting enough paper to wrap a house.

Before the surgery I had fulfilled my most important goal. The mantra I had repeated to myself on many long drives throughout the years finally came true. I bought my mom a beautiful house in Canada. It coincided with Christmas and my ma's birthday. The timing couldn't have been more perfect. Throughout the years I had offered to move my mom down to ol' Casa de Copeland in Tampa, but she said no. She's a Canadian through and through. For me, it was the greatest feeling in the world to finally be able to do this for her. It surpassed all of my personal and professional accomplishments to see the look on her face the first time she walked into her first, very own house. Any time

It surpassed all of my personal and professional accomplishments to see the look on her face the first time she walked into her first, very own house.

235

Backstage with James Hatfield and Dale Torborg (formerly The Demon of WCW).

I start to get discouraged about a match, story lines, or any personal hurdles, I think about that day and every problem seems trivial. I ended up spending the majority of my recovery time with her to furnish it, which was a lot of fun for me. The house came together nicely and I finally have my "hockey basement," adorned with everything Toronto Maple Leafs and New Jersey Devils. It is warm and cozy, and already feels just like home.

I also bought myself a guitar. I decided that since I now had the time, why not? It was a Gibson Les Paul voodoo series, my first but not my last. I have since become addicted and now own four-teen! Hey, I don't do anything half-assed! Maybe I went a little overboard, and real musicians will hate me, but it's good mental therapy (that's what I tell my accountant, anyway!). That little boy in the powder blue KISS Destroyer T-shirt and plastic guitar now has the real thing. All I needed was to learn how to play them, so I started taking lessons from my good friend Ty. I was on my way.

Hey, I don't do anything half-assed!

Throughout the year I was able to go to a lot of concerts. When you are on the road as much as we are, being able to go to concerts is some-times challenging, so I took full advantage. I

With Paul Stanley.

236

went to Metallica, Linkin Park, Limp Bizkit, KISS, Aerosmith, The Eagles, Poison, Vince Neil, Skid Row, Slayer, Stryper, Submersed, Fuel, Finger Eleven, etc., etc. I even got onstage with Skid Row and played a chord or two. Good thing I had started those lessons! One of the perks of my marginal "fame" is getting to meet other athletes and musicians. I was able to meet all of these bands, including KISS and Metallica. This was monumental for me. Metallica has been my musical muse since the eighties, and we all know how this kid feels about KISS. I met KISS with Jericho and later again with Hulk. That was pretty surreal. I was standing there in the Ice Palace in Tampa with my childhood heroes, KISS and Hulk Hogan. I can honestly say I *never* thought that would happen.

I tried to stay busy. It helped me to keep my mind off coming back and not getting too frustrated or depressed about my situation. Even though I was keeping busy, being home really opened my eyes to a lot of things. Alanah and I had been up and down so many times in our relationship. I used to think it was because I was on the road so much. Traveling as much as we do can be taxing on any relationship, but I always thought that if we could make it through my career until I retired we would eventually be all right. The only problem with that theory is that when I was home things got a lot worse. I tried to stay as positive as I could. I refused to admit the problems we were having on the home front were as bad as they were. We had been together for a long time, shared a lot of history and had a lot of ups and downs with each other, but sometimes that just isn't enough. Being at home didn't allow me to escape the feelings I had been having for a long time but didn't want to see or admit. I was happy everywhere else in my life, except at home. I had the surgery in March and in October I told Alanah I wanted a divorce. I really don't want to go into details of why and how our marriage fell apart, it just did. Sometimes things just are what they are. I came to realize that I was too young to be this miserable in what should have been the most important relationship in my life. I realized she was not the woman I wanted to

> Being at home didn't allow me to escape the feelings I had been having for a long time but didn't want to see or admit.

237

I felt sorry for myself and thought life had handed me a big steaming platter of horseshit.

spend the rest of my life with and couldn't ignore that feeling anymore. I am a loyal man who only wants to be happy, have children, play with my dogs, and enjoy the life I have been given. In case you are wondering, this decision did not affect my friendship with Sean at all.

On paper, the year was looking pretty bleak. There were times when I felt sorry for myself and thought life had handed me a big steaming platter of horseshit. I believe myself to be a positive person for the most part, but this was tough. Not only was I unsure about my future with WWE and my neck, I was now having to face the uncertainty of my future in my personal life as well. I guess the key is how you adapt to these situations to get you through the rough patches. I decided to take the horseshit and use it for fertilizer, helping me grow into the man I am today (yes, that means I am

Lisa.

full of shit!). That man is a much better, happier version of Adam Copeland.

At the time this was all taking place, the last thing that was on my mind was meeting someone else, but (just like the horseshit) you can't control what life hands you. That's when I met Lisa (I had actually met her three years prior, but we were both in other relationships and the meeting was simply a hello). She is a beautiful hybrid of nationalities ranging from Puerto Rican, Hawaiian, Chinese, German, and a few others. She walked into my life during a rough period, and somehow she was able to pull me through some of my most difficult times. It was like she hit me in the heart with a hammer lathered in love (oh yeah, the cheese meter just hit feta range, but I had to, it was too good not to use!).

I love my happy little unit. Lisa and my boys. My boys being a big, fun-loving yellow Lab named Luger (not named after the wrestler) and a teacup poodle named Branny. Yes, I have a poodle, but he's tough! With Lisa helping balance my personal life, I was able to focus on my comeback. It had been a long year, and an even longer road but it was almost time for my comeback.

Things were beginning to settle down and I was able to get focused on my comeback. Of course, like any good Edge story, there were bumps in the road and my comeback didn't go as smoothly as I had hoped it would. After getting my medical clearance from Dr. Youngblood, allowing me to get back into the ring, I was sent down to Ohio Valley Wrestling. OVW is our "farm system." Young guys go there to get groomed and guys like me go there to knock off the ring rust that settles in after taking eleven months off. I decided to drive to Louisville, Kentucky, where OVW is based, since I was going to be there for almost three weeks and would need a car (I thought it would be nice to have my own). It felt like I was making an indy trip again. Except for the fact that this time I was driving a Lexus SC430 instead of a run-down Econo-Van on its last legs. I arrived in Louisville after a day and a half and got right down to business. Within a week I was starting to feel like me again. My mind was ready, but my body wasn't. It was the beginning of my second week in OVW, and I was running some pretty easy drills, taking bumps, etc. At one point, I went to hit the ropes and turned my foot, spraining it. It started to swell up almost instantly and changed to a nice color mixture of green and

My mind was ready, but my body wasn't.

purple. I wasn't able to get in to see a doctor until the next day, where he then explained I had pulled and stretched just about every ligament and tendon in my right foot. By this time my foot had swollen to twice or maybe three

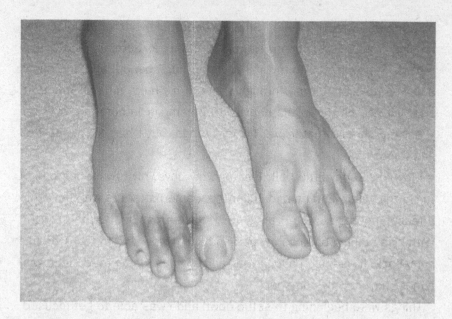

times its normal size (which is normally a fourteen) and was not a very pretty sight. There was not much the doctors could do for my foot. Basically, I was given a walking brace and told to stay off it for four to six weeks. I couldn't believe it! Lisa was back in Tampa when this happened so she flew up to Louisville to drive my gimpy ass back home.

So, there you have it. I had to take another month off to recoup the foot before heading back to OVW once again. On my first night back I wrestled in a match and broke my left hand. "What the hell is going on?" I thought to myself. I was starting to wonder if someone had a voodoo doll with my face on it. Either that or I just wasn't supposed to be in Louisville at that time. I could probably make it to the hospital blindfolded by now. When I got there they took X-rays and wrapped my hand in a nice bright red cast. My choice of colors were purple, red, or blue. Not exactly the most manly choices, not like a good black or camouflage cast. So now I had this big red cast on my left arm (that later faded, turning a dark shade of pink, which the guys ate up!). That's okay, and by now you should know my motto, "That which doesn't kill me, only makes me stronger!" And believe you me, I intend to stick around for a while!

Even with the foot not quite healed and the hand in a cast it was

> **I was starting to wonder if someone had a voodoo doll with my face on it.**

time to make my official comeback. It was time to inject new life into my character. I wanted my character to evolve again. A little older, a lot wiser, somewhat rested, with a definite chip on my shoulder and an angrier side that the fans hadn't seen from me yet. For

> The world championship . . . is a culmination of hard work and sacrifice.

lack of a better term, I wanted my character to gain more of an . . . edge. Coming back, I have one main goal in mind, and that is the world championship. Mick Foley said it best, "In our industry the world championship is the equivalent of winning the Oscar for best actor." It is a culmination of hard work and sacrifice. I won't be able to retire in contentment until I achieve it. I guess it's like Dan Marino or maybe Barry Bonds—with all of their great and personal accomplishments, it would've been nice for them to win the "big one." So that is what I'm shooting for. The Big One. Only I wouldn't be doing it on *SmackDown!*; instead, I was coming back to *Raw.*

Apparently it was quite an internal battle as to where I would end up. It was back and forth for some time. First I heard *Raw,* then *SmackDown!,* then *Raw* again. I felt *SmackDown!* needed the help more, what with the departures of Chris Benoit, Matt Hardy, and an injured Kurt Angle. *SmackDown!* also felt like my home. *Raw* was loaded with some big names but I was told RVD, Booker T, and the Dudleyz would be sent to *SmackDown!* to even things out. Finally, after meeting with Vince in New York, the decision was made and I was going to *Raw.* I looked at it as a great opportunity and a new set of challenges with a whole new set of opponents to wrestle.

> I can't wait to sink my teeth into a feud with Triple H, Randy Orton, Kane, Jericho, Jay, Batista, and another great, Ric Flair.

I can't wait to sink my teeth into a feud with Triple H, Randy Orton, Kane, Jericho, Jay, Batista, and another great, Ric Flair. Let's face it, every fan or wrestler has made a connection through Ric Flair International Wrestling airport. He is a legend and I find it an honor to be able to work with him. I can't wait for him to teach me how to be the man.

I've always looked up to Shawn Michaels and patterned my style

You can hear Randy thinking,
"nice pink cast."

after him. I would love to team with him. Better yet, I would love to stand across the ring from him. My final wish for an opponent would be Chris Benoit. I was at Lisa's stepmom's house in Denver when I watched him win the world title at *WrestleMania XX*. Immediately, I pictured Edge vs. Benoit in an Iron Man match. That would be great.

Before I could make any of my dream matches come true, I had to make my official comeback in my old stomping grounds: Motor City! Detroit would be the place. I was in Canada celebrating at a huge birthday party for my grandparents when I got the call telling me my presence was required the following Monday in Detroit. This was not the original plan, but *Raw* was hosting a draft lottery and some new faces were being changed between the shows. My ugly mug being one of them. I thought I would have a couple of weeks before my official comeback, scheduled for *Backlash* in Edmonton, but it was moved up to the draft at *Raw*. Only one of the vignettes promoting my comeback had time to air before I was back in the mix. It may have

Here I am with my cousins Matt, Shannon, Kyle, and Chris, celebrating my grandparents' birthday.

been rushed, and I wasn't exactly pleased, but that's life in the wrestling biz.

In case you were wondering what was going through my mind after having thirteen months off, my laundry list of injuries, and a divorce, here is a rare glimpse into my daily journal the day of my comeback.

I was back in the mix. It may have been rushed, and I wasn't exactly pleased, but that's life in the wrestling biz.

Journal Entry

March 22, 2004: 7:07 A.M./Tampa

I'm up, I'm up. Nervous energy woke me up. I actually had a dream that my music was playing over and over and I was nowhere to be found. Vince was pitching a fit and said "You're fiiirrrreee . . ." and I woke up. Shave, shower, breakfast, and I'm off to Motown.

9:08 A.M./Tampa airport

At the gate after a steady diet of Sevendust and Damageplan on my way to the airport. Keep replaying how the crowd will react in my mind. Can't wait to get out in front of them again.

11:22 A.M./en route to Detroit

On the plane. Seat 3D. The fact that the first thing I thought of when I saw my seat number was the Dudleyz and the crowd yelling 3D, is probably a sign that I have too much wrestling on the brain. It's a disease. Finished four crosswords and set to read The Juror by John Grisham.

6:14 P.M./Joe Louis Arena

Sitting in the dressing room with Jay, Jericho, Rey, Kidman, Matt, Chioda, and Lance. It's been fun to see everyone. Definitely amped for tonight. Spearing Eric Bischoff and the comeback begins. A year of pent-up frustration. I should apologize to Eric beforehand. In the lottery I officially become a member of <u>Raw</u>. I'll miss Kurt, Eddie, Doug, Rey, and the boys, but I'm looking forward to some new challenges. The second half of my career starts tonight.

10:00 P.M.

The time is drawing near. Ready as I'm gonna get. Hope the foot doesn't give out. I think I could do it with two stumps right now. Right now Book and RVD are on their way to the ring. Nervous anticipation. I hope the crowd reacts the way I want them to. They sound a little flat. Hopefully I can get them up. Here goes.

11:24 P.M.

Done! Man, what a feeling. Every frustration of the last year evaporated. When the sun finally sets on my career it will be tough, but I will fondly remember this night. Thank you, Motor City, thank you. Eric is okay, even though I drove him into the turnbuckles. Foot hurt, but adrenaline drove me through. Wasn't exactly the way I pictured my comeback, but you make the most of what is written. So begins the second chapter of my career.

March 23, 2004: 2:18 A.M.

Just hit bed after a nutritious meal of two quarter pounders with cheese. Nothing like McDonald's at 1:30 A.M. to celebrate. Ahh, back on the road, and the glamorous life of a pro wrestler.

My grin says it all.

Well, that's it. The end of the line. The whole enchilada. Adios, amigos! Sayonara. G'day eh (Canadian). The comeback is well under way. In fact, while we were editing this bad boy, I won tag titles for the tenth time, this time with Chris Benoit, tying the all-time record. I also added my fifth I-C title reign by beating a great new opponent and rival, Randy Orton. I have a feeling we will be seeing this one for a long time to come. But I'll save these details for my second book! My neck feels great and seems to be holding up better than ever. My foot and hand improve daily and are almost completely healed. It looks like a heel turn is in my future. Our crowd, ultimately, makes that decision, and if that's the case, I can't wait. I wrestle better as a 'face, but it is much more fun (and easier) to piss people off. Professionally, I am excited, anxious, and feel as though I'm on top of the world. Personally, after walking through a thunderstorm, I have found the pot of gold at the end of the rainbow (that's you, Lisa!). My mom is taken care of, cuddled up in her cozy house. The dogs are as happy as ever. Things are pretty good in Adam Copeland's corner of the world. Looking back, I didn't always think they would be, but things always have a way of working out. One door shuts, another one opens.

Before I go, I wanted to tell each and every one of you, "Thank you." Thank you for reading this. Thank you for your kind words on the streets, in shopping malls, and in restaurants. It really helped to have the fans' support. I hope you had as much fun reading this as I had writing it. This book is yet another dream realized. Only one "big one" left to go. You know what it is. Hope you don't mind coming along and enjoying the rest of my ride!

ACKNOWLEDGMENTS

jump around in tights in front of thousands of people for WWE every night. As you now know, that was always my dream. Many people helped me to get here, and many people have helped me succeed here.

First I would like to thank my Ma for her unwavering support and love, which molded me into the man I am today.

To my grandparents and the rest of the Copeland clan, I love you.

The "Getalong Gang": John John, who saves lives as a paramedic; Johnny, who now paints his visions for museums across Canada; Fatty, who now drives twenty hours for fifty dollars as he pays his dues the old-fashioned way on the indy wrestling circuit as Sinn; and—of course—there's Jay. (What a story. We actually did it, buddy. In life, you are the brother I never had. On TV, the brother I do have.) To all of the "gang," for all the laughter, the history we've created, and the memories we've shared, thanks.

To the Resos, I want everyone to know you are my second family.

I've been blessed to have some of the best ever in this business grace me with their knowledge. My first trainers were Sweet Daddy Siki and Ron Hutchinson. Then there was the priceless advice of Bret Hart, Leo Burke, Dory Funk, Jr., Tom Prichard, Michael Hayes, Pat Patterson, John Laurinaitis, Fit Finlay, Arn Anderson, William Regal, Dean Malenko, Steve Keirn, Jack Lanza, Tony, Garea, Bad News Allen (Brown), and Gerry Morrow.

I want to thank Tony Condello and Don Callus for giving me the outlet to cut my teeth in this industry.

Rhyno (no, I never call him Terry), along with Jay, you are my best friend in the business.

My fellow road warriors, Swinger, Keith, Joe, Rob, and Scott. Can you believe the places we went together?

Sean, we both made it.

To Ric Flair and Hulk Hogan, I want to thank you for making this kid the happiest he's ever been inside a wrestling ring.

To my "fellow author" and partner in TV tomfoolery, Mick Foley, thanks for all your support and encouragement.

These people have been some of my favorite opponents and partners, and they are also some of my closest friends: Chris Benoit, Eddie Guerrero, Kurt Angle, Chris Jericho, Lance Storm, Test, Rey Mysterio, Randy Orton, and of course the Hardys, Lita and Dudleys. Thanks for the history.

Matt Smith, thank you for keeping the IRS at bay. And to Ed Koskey, my lawyer, I appreciate all your advice and support.

Simon & Schuster and Stacey Pascarella actually believed I could do this.

The McMahons, Carl DeMarco, and all of the WWE staff gave me the opportunity to realize my dream.

And finally Lisa. You are my partner, my best friend, the shoulder I lean on, my sympathetic ear. I can't wait to start our life together.

Printed in the USA
CPSIA information can be obtained
at www.ICGtesting.com
LVHW031737271123
765061LV00018B/919